The Language of Flowers: The Floral Offering

Henrietta Dumont

BIBLIOLIFE

THE

FLORAL OFFERING:

A

TOKEN OF AFFECTION AND ESTEEM;.

COMPRISING

The Language and Poetry of Flowers.

WITH COLOURED ILLUSTRATIONS, FROM ORIGINAL DRAWINGS.

By HENRIETTA DUMONT.

PHILADELPHIA:
H. C. PECK & THEO. BLISS.
1852.

Preface.

WHY has the beneficent Creator scattered over the face of the earth such a profusion of beautiful flowers—flowers by the thousand and million, in every land—from the tiny snowdrop that gladdens the chill spring of the north, to the gorgeous magnolia that flaunts in the sultry regions of the tropics? Why is it that every landscape has its appropriate flowers, every nation its national flowers, every rural home its home flowers? Why do flowers enter and shed their perfume over every scene of life, from the cradle to the grave? Why are flowers made to utter all voices of joy and sorrow in all varying scenes, from the chaplet that adorns the bride to the votive wreath that blooms over the tomb?

5

It is for no other reason than that flowers have in themselves a real and natural significance. They have a positive relation to man, his sentiments, passions, and feelings. They correspond to actual emotions. They have their mission—a mission of love and mercy. They have their language, and from the remotest ages this language has found its interpreters.

In the East the language of flowers has been universally understood and applied "time out of mind." Its meaning finds a place in their poetry and in all their literature, and it is familiarly known among the people. In Europe it has existed and been recognised for long ages among the people, although scarcely noticed by the literati until a comparatively recent period. Shakspeare, however, whom nothing escaped which was known to the people, exhibits his intimate acquaintance with the language of flowers in his masterly delineation of the madness of Ophelia.

Recent writers in all languages recognise the beauty and propriety of this language to such an extent, that an acquaintance with it has now become indispensable as a part of a polished education.

Our little volume is devoted to the explanation
of this beautiful language.   We have made it as
complete as our materials and limits would permit.
We present it to our readers in the humble hope
that we shall increase the means of elegant and
innocent enjoyment by our "Floral Offering."

Contents.

Contents.

The Floral Offering.

MEZEREON....*Coquetry—Desire to please.*

THIS shrub, clothed in its showy garb, appears
amidst the snow, like an imprudent and coquettish
female, who, though shivering with cold, wears her
spring attire in the depth of winter. The stalk of this
shrub is covered with a dry bark, which gives it the
appearance of dead wood. Nature, to hide this de-
formity, has encircled each of its sprays with a wreath
of red flowers, terminating in a tuft of leaves. These
flowers give out a peculiar and offensive smell.

You oftentimes can mark upon the street
  The gilded toy whom fashion idolizes;
Heartless and fickle, swelled with self-conceit,
  Avoiding alway what good sense advises.
Who flutters like the butterfly while burns his sun,
Nor afterwards is missed when life is done.

W. H. C.

Clouds turn with every wind about;
They keep us in suspense and doubt;
Yet oft perverse, like woman-kind,
Are seen to scud against the wind.
Is not this lady just the same?
For who can tell what is her aim?

Swift.

Thou delightest the cold world's gaze,
   When crowned with the flower and the gem,
But thy lover's smile should be dearer praise
   Than the incense thou prizest from them.
And gay is the playful tone,
   As to the flattering voice thou respondest;
But what is the praise of the cold and unknown
   To the tender blame of the fondest?

John Everett.

Know, Celia, (since thou art so proud,)
   'Twas I that gave thee thy renown:
Thou hadst, in the forgotten crowd
   Of common beauties, lived unknown,
Had not my verse exhaled thy name,
And with it impt the wings of Fame.
That killing power is none of thine,
   I gave it to thy voice and eyes:
Thy sweets, thy graces, all are mine;
   Thou art my star, shin'st in my skies!
Then dart not from thy borrowed sphere
Lightning on him that fixed thee there.

Thomas Carew.

SNOWDROP....*Hope.*

THE Snowdrop is looked upon as the herald of the approach of flower-wreathed Spring. The north winds howl; the naked branches of the trees are white with frost; the earth is carpeted with the virgin snow; the feathered musicians are silent; and stern Winter's icy hand chills the rivulet till it ceases to murmur. At this season, a tender flower springs up amid the snow, expands its blossoms, and leads thought to the verdant hours to come. This beautiful sign of awakening Nature may aptly be considered as the emblem of Hope.

The Snowdrop, winter's timid child,
　Awakes to life bedewed with tears,
And flings around its fragrance mild;
And, where no rival flowerets bloom,
Amidst the bare and chilling gloom
　A beauteous gem appears.
All weak and wan, with head inclined,
　Its parent breast the drifted snow,
It trembles, while the ruthless wind
Bends its slim form; the tempest lowers,
Its emerald eye drops crystal showers
　On its cold bed below.
Where'er I find thee, gentle flower,
　Thou still art sweet and dear to me;
For I have known the cheerless hour,
Have seen the sunbeams cold and pale,
Have felt the chilling wintry gale,
　And wept and shrunk, like thee!

Mary Robinson.

No one is so accursed by fate,
No one so utterly desolate,
  But some heart, though unknown,
  Responds unto his own;
Responds, as if with unseen wings
An angel touched its quivering strings,
  And whispers in its song,
  "Where hast thou stayed so long?"
                  Longfellow.

The star of Hope will beam in Sorrow's night,
And smile the phantoms of Despair to flight.
                  Anon.

"Why do you call the Snowdrop pale,
  Our first of flowerets bright?
For the Christmas Rose came long before,
  So did the Aconite."
I know the yellow Aconite;
  I know the Christmas Rose:
But neither one nor other e'er
  Within my garden grows.
They seem to me presumptuous things,
  That rudely hurry on,
And struggle for the precedence
  A fairer flower hath won.
When I was but a wee, wee thing,
  A young Snowdrop I nursed,
And I loved it when they told me how
  It always blossomed first.
I marked its tiny, trembling stem,
  And dainty little bell,

And, oh! so tenderly enjoyed
  Its faint, delicious smell.
It was not only fair and sweet,
  'Twas the first flower that came;
So said they then, and there is none
  I could love now the same.
The Aconite may deck with gold
  Its merry little face—
The Christmas Rose at Christmas bloom,
  But none can fill *her* place.
Within my garden's small domain
  The Snowdrop still shall find
Herself the earliest flower.   She leads,
  The others come behind.
And, lo! above the heaving mould
  The clustering bells hang here;
Like foam upon the storm-black wave,
  Or pearls in Ethiop's ear.
And I know where they're crowding thick,
  With none their wealth to note;—
All o'er that woody isle, that lies
  Girt by the ancient moat.
There, under tall, dark crested firs,
  The Snowdrops spring each year;
And shed about that gloomy place
  A lightness pale and clear.
A grand old Manor House once stood
  On that dim moated isle;
But long years since have floated by,
  And its story died the while.
Yet roses, cultured ones, run wild,
  And fruits, grown rough and sour.

2

That linger still around, tell tales
     Of garden and of bower.
And so the Snowdrops may have dwelt
     In borders neat and trim,
And gentle beings tended them,
     Though now all's drear and dim.
The brave and beautiful have died,
     Not e'en a name is known :—
Time hath laid low the stately house,—
     Ye cannot find a stone.
But still there runneth brightly there
     The little sedgy stream
Into the moat, that lieth still
     And shadowy as a dream.
And still there groweth plenteously
     The fragile Snowdrop's bell :—
Oh, human pride! that thou wouldst list
     The tale these small things tell!
                    Louisa A. Twamley.

As Hope, with bowed head, silent stood,
     And on her golden anchor leant,
Watching below the angry flood,
     While Winter, mid the dreariment
Half-buried in the drifted snow,
     Lay sleeping on the frozen ground,
Not heeding how the wind did blow,
     Bitter and bleak on all around :
She gazed on Spring, who at her feet
Was looking on the snow and sleet.
Spring sighed, and through the driving gale
     Her warm breath caught the falling snow.

And from the flakes a flower as pale
  Did into spotless whiteness blow.
Hope, smiling, saw the blossom fall,
  And watched its root strike in the earth:
"I will that flower the Snowdrop call,"
  Said Hope, "in memory of its birth:
And through all ages it shall be
In reverence held, for love of me."
"And ever from my hidden bowers,"
  Said Spring, "it first of all shall go,
And be the herald of the flowers,
  To warn away the sheeted snow.
Its mission done, then by thy side
  All summer long it shall remain.
While other flowers I scatter wide,
  O'er every hill, and wood, and plain,
This shall return, and ever be
A sweet companion, Hope, for thee."
Hope stooped and kissed her sister Spring,.
  And said, "For hours, when thou art gone,
I'm left alone without a thing
  That I can fix my heart upon:
'Twill cheer me many a lonely hour,
  And in the future I shall see
Those who would sink raised by that flower;
  They'll look on it, then think of thee:
And many a sadful heart shall sing,
  Tho Snowdrop bringeth Hope and Spring."
Miller.

PRIMROSE....*Early Grief.*

THE Primrose is one of the earliest flowers of spring. It was anciently called Paralisos, the name of a beautiful youth, who died of grief for the loss of his betrothed Melicerta, and was metamorphosed by his parents into this flower, which has since been a favourite of the poets.

> With fairest flowers,
> Whilst summer last, and I live here, Fidele,
> I'll sweeten thy sad grave: thou shalt not lack
> The flower that's like thy face, pale Primrose.
> > *Cymbeline.*

The Primrose pale is Nature's meek and modest child.
> *Balfour.*

> Nay, weep not while thy sun shines bright,
>   And cloudless is thy day,
> While past and present joys unite
>   To cheer thee on thy way;
> While fond companions round thee move,
>   To youth and nature true,
> And friends whose looks of anxious love
>   Thy every step pursue.
> > *Common-Place Book of Poetry.*

> The Primrose, tenant of the glade,
> Emblem of virtue in the shade.
> > *John Mayne.*

Ask me why I send you here
This firstling of the infant year;
Ask me why I send to you
This Primrose all bepearled with dew:
I straight will whisper in your ears,
The sweets of love are washed with tears.
Ask me why this flower doth show
So yellow, green, and sickly too;
Ask me why the stalk is weak
And bending, yet it doth not break:
I must tell you these discover
What doubts and fears are in a lover.

Thomas Carew.

By the soft green light in the woody glade,
On the banks of moss where thy childhood played,
By the household tree through which thine eye
First looked in love to the summer sky;
By the dewy gleam, by the very breath
Of the Primrose-tufts in the grass beneath,
Upon thy heart there is laid a spell,
Holy and precious—oh, guard it well!
Yes! when thy heart in its pride would stray
From the first pure loves of its youth away;
When the sullying breath of the world would come
O'er the flowers it brought from its native home;
Think thou again of the woody glade,
Of the sound by the rustling ivy made;
Think of the tree at thy father's door,
And the kindly spell shall have power once more.

Mrs. Hemans.

ALMOND BLOSSOM....*Indiscretion.*

THE Almond tree is the first of the trees to put forth
its blossoms, when spring breathes the breath of life
through nature. It has been made the emblem of in-
discretion, from flowering so early that frosts too often
give a death-chill to the precocious germs of its fruit.
In ancient times, the abundance of blossoms upon the
Almond tree was considered to promise a fruitful season. The following is the fabulous account of the origin
of this tree:—Demophoon, son of Theseus and Phædra,
in returning from the siege of Troy, was thrown by a
storm on the shores of Thrace, where then reigned the
beautiful Phyllis. The young queen graciously received the prince, fell in love with him, and became his
wife. When recalled to Athens by his father's death,
Demophoon promised to return in a month, and fixed
the day. The loving Phyllis counted the hours of his
absence, and, at last, the appointed day arrived. Nine
times she repaired to the shore; but, losing all hope
of his return, she died of grief, and was converted into
an Almond tree. Soon afterwards, Demophoon returned. Overwhelmed with sorrow, he offered a sacri-
fice at the sea-side, to appease the manes of his bride.
The Almond tree instantly put forth its blossoms, and
seemed to sympathize with his repentance.

> Oh! had I nursed when I was young
> The lessons of my father's tongue,
> (The deep laborious thoughts he drew
> From all he saw, and others knew,)

I might have been,—ah, me!
Thrice sager than I e'er shall be.
       For what says Time?
Alas! he only shows the truth
Of all that I was told in youth.
                Barry Cornwall.

CROCUS.... *Youth.*

THE Crocus is one of the earliest of the spring flowers, and, therefore, a fit emblem of the spring of life.
It is a small flower, of variegated hues; the principal
being purple, yellow, and white. The *Crocus Vernus,*
or Spring Crocus, is a wild flower now in various parts
of England, though not considered to be really a native
of the country. We learn from the favourite writers,
Mr. and Mrs. Howitt, that they are plentiful about
Nottingham, "gleaming at a distance like a perfect
flood of lilac, and tempting very many little hearts, and
many graver ones too, to go out and gather."

Oh! many a glorious flower there grows
   In far and richer lands;
But high in my affection e'er
   The beautiful Crocus stands.
I love their faces, when by one
   And two they're looking out;
I love them when the spreading field
   Is purple all about.
I loved them in the by-gone years
   Of childhood's thoughtless laughter,
When I marvelled why the flowers came first,
   And the leaves the season after.

I loved them then, I love them now—
   The gentle and the bright;
I love them for the thoughts they bring
   Of spring's returning light;
When, first-born of the waking earth,
   Their kindred gay appear,
And, with the Snowdrop, usher in
   The hope-invested year.

                 Louisa A. Twamley.

       You're glad
Because your little tiny nose,
   Turns up so pert and funny;
Because I know you choose your beaux
   More for their mirth than money;
Because your eyes are deep and blue,—
   Your fingers long and rosy;
Because a little maid like you
   Would make one's home so cozy;
Because, I think, (I'm just so weak,)
   That some of these fine morrows
You'll listen while you hear me speak
   My story, and *my* sorrows!

                 Anon.

Gay hope is theirs, by fancy fed,
Less pleasing when possest;
The tear forgot as soon as shed,
The sunshine of the breast;
Theirs buxom health, of rosy hue;
Wild wit, invention ever new,
And lively cheer of vigour born;

The thoughtless day, the easy night,
The spirits pure, the slumbers light,
That fly the approach of morn.
Alas, regardless of their doom,
The little victims play !
No sense have they of ills to come,
No care beyond to-day.
Yet see how all around them wait,
The ministers of human fate,
And black misfortune's baleful train,
Ah ! show them where in ambush stand,
To seize their prey, the murderous band!
Ah, tell them they are men !

Gray's Eton College.

Life went a Maying
With Nature, Hope, and Poesy,
When I was young !

Coleridge.

ICE-PLANT....*Frigidity.*

Canst thou no kindly ray impart,
  Thou strangely beauteous one?
Fairer than fairest work of art,
  Yet cold as sculptured stone!
Thou art in Friendship's bright domain
  A flower that yields no fruit;
And Love declares thy beauty vain ;—
  Of fragrance destitute !

O. S. M. Ordway.

With pellucid studs the Ice-Flower gems
His rimy foliage, and his candied stems.

Darwin.

As water fluid is, till it do grow
  Solid and fixed by cold,
So in warm seasons love doth loosely flow;
  Frost only can it hold;
    Your coldness and disdain
    Does the sweet course restrain.

Cowley.

CACTUS....*Ardent Love.*

THE flower of the Cactus is chosen to signify ardent
love, because of the glowing hues of the flower itself,
and the heat of the climate in which the plant grows
to the greatest size. The gorgeousness of the flower
of the Cactus needs no eulogy. No fitter emblem could
have been selected to represent the passion of love in
its full flame.

I think of thee, when soft and wide
  The evening spreads her robes of light,
And, like a young and timid bride,
  Sits blushing in the arms of night:
And when the moon's sweet crescent springs
  In light o'er heaven's deep waveless sea,
And stars are forth like blessed things,
  I think of thee—I think of thee.

G. W. Prentice.

Thou'rt like a star; for when my way was cheerless
    and forlorn,
And all was blackness like the sky before a coming
    storm,
Thy beaming smile and words of love, thy heart of
    kindness free,
Illumed my path, then cheered my soul, and bade its
    sorrows flee.
Thou'rt like a star—when sad and lone I wander forth
    to view
The lamps of night, beneath their rays my spirit's
    nerved anew,
And thus I love to gaze on thee, and then I think
    thou'st power
To mix the cup of joy for me, even in life's darkest
    hour.
Thou'rt like a star—whene'er my eye is upward turned
    to gaze
Upon those orbs, I mark with awe their clear celestial
    blaze;
And then thou seem'st so pure, so high, so beautifully
    bright,
I almost feel as if it were an *angel* met my sight.
American Ladies' Magazine.

Could genius sink in dull decay,
And wisdom cease to lend her ray;
Should all that I have worshipped change,
Even this could not my heart estrange;
Thou still wouldst be the first, the first
That taught the love sad tears have nursed.
Mrs. Embury.

The sick soul

That burns with love's delusions, ever dreams,
Dreading its losses. It for ever makes
A gloomy shadow gather in the skies,
And clouds the day; and looking far beyond
The glory in its gaze, it sadly sees
Countless privations, and far-coming storms,
Shrinking from what it conjures.

Simms's Poems.

The rolling wheel, that runneth often round,
The hardest steel in tract of time doth tear;
And drizzling drops, that often do redound,
Firmest flint doth in continuance wear:
Yet cannot I, with many a dropping tear,
And long entreaty, soften her hard heart,
That she will once vouchsafe my plaint to hear,
Or look with pity on my painful smart:
But when I plead, she bids me play my part;
And when I weep, she says tears are but water;
And when I sigh, she says I know the art;
And when I wail, she turns herself to laughter;
So do I weep and wail, and plead in vain,
While she as steel and flint doth still remain.

Spenser.

Aloe.... *Grief.*

THE Aloe is attached to the soil by very feeble roots;
it delights to grow in the wilderness, and its taste is
extremely bitter. Thus grief separates us from earthly
things, and fills the heart with bitterness. These mag-

nificent and monstrous plants are found in barbarous
Africa: they grow upon rocks, in dry sand under a
burning atmosphere. Some have leaves six feet long,
and armed with long spires. From the centre of these
leaves shoots up a slender stem covered with flowers.

Sister Sorrow! sit beside me,
Or, if I must wander, guide me:
Let me take thy hand in mine,
Cold alike are mine and thine.
Think not, Sorrow, that I hate thee,—
Think not I am frightened at thee,—
Thou art come for some good end;
I will treat thee as a friend.

R. M. Milnes.

And this is all I have left now,
    Silence and solitude and tears;
The memory of a broken vow,
    My blighted hopes, my wasted years!

Anon.

It may be that I shall forget my grief;
    It may be time has good in store for me;
It may be that my heart will find relief
    From sources now unknown. Futurity
May bear within its folds some hidden spring
    From which will issue blessed streams; and yet
Whate'er of joy the coming year may bring,
    The past—the past—I never can forget.

Mrs. Hale.

Of comfort no man speak:
Let's talk of graves, of worms, of epitaphs:
Make dust our paper, and with rainy eyes
Write sorrow on the bosom of the earth.
Let's choose executors, and talk of wills;
And yet not so—for what can we bequeath,
Save our deposed bodies in the ground?

Shakspeare.

WORMWOOD....*Absence.*

WORMWOOD is the bitterest of plants; and absence, according to La Fontaine, is the worst of evils. Those in whose anxious breasts the "flame divine" is burning, will agree with the French author in his assertion. To be absent from one we love is to carry a vacant chamber in the heart, which naught else can fill.

When thou shalt yield to memory's power,
And let her fondly lead thee o'er
The scenes that thou hast past before,
To absent friends and days gone by,—
Then should these meet thy pensive eye,
A true memento may they be
Of one whose bosom owes to thee
So many hours enjoyed in gladness,
That else perhaps had passed in sadness,
And many a golden dream of joy,
Untarnished and without alloy.
Oh, still my fervent prayer will be,
"Heaven's choicest blessings rest on thee."

Miss Gould.

How can the glintin sun shine bright?
How can the wimplin burnie glide?
Or flowers adorn the ingle side?
    Or birdies deign
The woods, and streams, and vales to chide?
    Eliza's gane!

                      J. W. H.

If she be gone, the world, in my esteem,
Is all bare walls; nothing remains in it
But dust and feathers.

                      John Crown.

Thus absence dies, and dying proves
No absence can subsist with loves
    That do partake of fair perfection;
Since, in the darkest night, they may,
By love's quick motion, find a way
    To see each other in reflection.

                      Suckling.

VIOLET....*Modest Worth.*

THE Violet has always been a favourite theme of admiration among visitors of Parnassus. Its quiet beauty and love of retired spots have ever made it the emblem of true worth that shrinks from parade. It is one of the first children of spring, and awakens pleasing emotions in the breast of the lover of the beautiful, as he strolls through the meadows in the season of joy. Ion, the Greek name of this flower, is traced by some etymologists to Ia, the daughter of Midas, who was be-

trothed to Atys, and changed by Diana into a Violet,
to hide her from Apollo.

A woman's love, deep in the heart,
  Is like the Violet flower,
That lifts its modest head apart
  In some sequestered bower.

Anon.

The maid whose manners are retired,
Who, patient, waits to be admired,
Though overlooked, perhaps, a while
Her modest worth, her modest smile,—
Oh, she will find, or soon, or late,
A noble, fond, and faithful mate,
Who, when the spring of life is gone,
And all its blooming flowers are flown,
Will bless old Time, who left behind
The graces of a virtuous mind.

Paulding.

Pansies, Lilies, Kingcups, Daisies,
Let them live upon their praises;
Long as there's a sun that sets,
  Primroses will have their glory;
Long as there are Violets,
  They will have a place in story:
There's a flower that shall be mine,
'Tis the little Celandine.
Eyes of some men travel far
For the finding of a star;
Up and down the heavens they go,
  Men that keep a mighty rout!

I'm as great as they, I trow,
  Since the day I found thee out,
Little flower!—I'll make a stir,
Like a great astronomer.
Modest, yet withal an elf,
Bold, and lavish of thyself,
Since we needs must first have met
  I have seen thee, high and low,
Thirty years or more, and yet
  'Twas a face I did not know:
Thou hast now, go where I may,
Fifty greetings in a day.
Ere a leaf is on the bush,
In the time before the thrush
Has a thought about its nest,
  Thou wilt come with half a call,
Spreading out thy glossy breast
  Like a careless prodigal;
Telling tales about the sun,
When there's little warmth or none.

              Wordsworth.

Shakspeare regarded the Violet as the emblem of constancy, as the following occurs in one of his sonnets:—

Violet is for faithfulness,
  Which in me shall abide;
Hoping, likewise, that from your heart
  You will not let it slide.

              Shakspeare.

The Violet in her greenwood bower,
  Where birchen boughs with hazles mingle,
May boast herself the fairest flower,
  In glen, or copse, or forest dingle.

Scott.

Under the hedge all safe and warm,
Sheltered from boisterous wind and storm,
    We Violets lie:
    With each small eye
Closely shut while the cold goes by.
You look at the bank, mid the biting frost,
And you sigh, and say that we're dead and lost;
    But, Lady stay
    For a sunny day,
And you'll find us again, alive and gay.
On mossy banks, under forest trees,
You'll find us crowding, in days like these;
    Purple and blue,
    And white ones too,
Peep at the sun, and wait for you.
By maids and matrons, by old and young,
By rich and poor, our praise is sung;
    And the blind man sighs
    When his sightless eyes
He turns to the spot where our perfumes rise.
There is not a garden, the country through,
Where they plant not Violets, white and blue;
    By princely hall,
    And cottage small—
For we're sought, and cherished, and culled by all.

Yet grand parterres and stiff trimmed beds
But ill become our modest heads;
    We'd rather run,
    In shadow and sun,
O'er the banks where our merry lives first begun.
There, where the Birken bough's silvery shine
Gleams over the hawthorn and frail woodbine,
    Moss, deep and green,
    Lies thick, between
The plots where we Violet-flowers are seen.
And the small gay Celandine's stars of gold
Rise sparkling beside our purple's fold:—
    Such a regal show
    Is rare, I trow,
Save on the banks where Violets grow.
Louisa A. Twamley.

I know where bloom some Violets in a bed
    Half hidden in the grass; and crowds go by
    And see them not, unless some curious eye
Unto their hiding-place by chance is led.
    I often pass that way, and look on them,
And love them more and more. I know not why
My heart doth love such humble things; but I
    Esteem them more than robe or diadem
Of haughty kings. A babe, or bird, or flower
Hath o'er the soul a most despotic power.
    The tearful eye of infancy oppressed—
A flower down-trodden by the foot of spite—
    Awaken sighs of sorrow in the breast,
Or nerve the arm to vindicate their right.
MacKellar.

LAVENDER....*Distrust.*

IT was anciently believed that the asp, a dangerous species of viper, made Lavender its habitual place of abode, for which reason that plant was approached with extreme caution. The Romans used it largely in their baths, from whence its name is derived.

> Our doubts are traitors,
> And make us lose the good we oft might win,
> By fearing to attempt.
> *Shakspeare.*

> Who never doubted never half believed,
> Where doubt there truth is—'tis her shadow.
> *Bailey.*

> When first, with all a lover's pride,
> I wooed and won thee for my bride,
> I little thought that thou couldst be
> Estranged as now thou art from me !
> *Anon.*

> Thy confidence is held from me,
>   In fear my love but shows,
> Like one, art thou, who fears the bee
>   May sting thee, through the rose.
> *Anon.*

PANSY....*Think of me.*

THE Pansy, or Heart's-ease, is a beautiful variety of
the Violet, differing from it in the diversity of its colours. In fragrance it is inferior to the Violet. Pansy
is an old English corruption of the French Pensée.

And there are Pansies, that's for thoughts."
                                        Shakspeare.

CHILDHOOD.

Sister, arise, the sun shines bright,
  The bee is humming in the air,
The stream is singing in the light,
  The May-buds never looked more fair;
Blue is the sky, no rain to-day:
  Get up, it has been light for hours,
And we have not begun to play,
  Nor have we gathered any flowers.
Time, who looked on, each accent caught,
And said, "He is too young for thought."

YOUTH.

To-night, beside the garden-gate?
  Oh, what a while the night is coming!
I never saw the sun so late,
  No heard the bee at this time humming!
I thought the flowers an hour ago
  Had closed their bells and sunk to rest:
How slowly flies that hooded crow!
  How light it is along the west!
Said Time, "He yet hath to be taught
That I oft move too quick for thought."

MANHOOD.

What thoughts wouldst thou in me awaken?
  Not love? for that brings only tears—
Nor friendship? no, I was forsaken!
  Pleasure I have nöt known for years:
The future I would not foresee,
  I know too much from what is past,
No happiness is there for me,
  And troubles ever come too fast.
Said Time, "No comfort have I brought,
The past to him's one painful thought."

OLD AGE.

Somehow the flowers seem different now,
  The Daisies dimmer than of old;
There's fewer blossoms on the bough,
  The Hawthorn buds look gray and cold;
The Pansies wore another dye
  When I was young—when I was young!
There's not that blue about the sky
  Which every way in those days hung.
There's nothing now looks as it "ought."
Said Time, "The change is in thy thought."

Miller.

I think of thee at morn, when glisten
  The tearful dew-drops on the grass;
I think of thee at eve, and listen,
  When the low, whispering breezes pass.

E. R. H.

And thou, so rich in gentle names, appealing
To hearts that own our nature's common lot;
Thou, styled by sportive Fancy's better feeling
A Thought, the Heart's-Ease, and Forget-me-not.

Barton.

Daisy....*Innocence.*

SHAKSPEARE speaks of the Daisy as the flower

Whose white investments figure innocence;

and succeeding poets have generally used it as the
image of that pure quality. Fable informs us that the
Daisy owes its origin to Belides, one of the Dryads,
who were supposed to preside over meadows and pastures. While dancing on the turf with Ephigeus,
whose suit she encouraged, she attracted the admiration of Vertumnus, the deity who presided over orchards;
and, to escape from him, she was transformed into the
humble flower, the Latin name of which is Bellis. The
ancient English name of the flower was Day's Eye, of
which Daisy is a corruption. In Ossian's poems, the
Daisy is called the flower of the new-born—most expressive of innocence.

When smitten by the morning ray,
I see thee rise alert and gay,
Then, cheerful flower! my spirits play
    With kindred gladness:
And when, at dark, by dews opprest,
Thou sink'st, the image of thy rest
Hath often eased my pensive breast
    Of careful sadness.

Wordsworth.

She dwells amid the world's dark ways,
    Pure as in childhood's hours;
And all her thoughts are poetry,
    And all her words are flowers.
                        Mrs. M. E. Hewitt.

'Twas when the world was in its prime,
    When meadows green and woodlands wild
Were strewn with flowers, in sweet spring-time,
    And everywhere the Daisies smiled.
When undisturbed the ring-doves cooed,
    While lovers sang each other's praises,
As in embowered lanes they wooed,
    Or on some bank white o'er with Daisies:
While Love went by with muffled feet,
Singing, "The Daisies they are sweet."
Unfettered then he roamed abroad,
    And as he willed it past the hours—
Now lingering idly by the road,
    Now loitering by the wayside flowers;
For what cared he about the morrow?
    Too young to sigh, too old to fear—
No time had he to think of sorrow,
    Who found the Daisies everywhere;
Still sang he, through each green retreat,
"The Daisies they are very sweet."
With many a maiden did he dally,
    Like a glad brook that turns away—
Here in, there out, across the valley,
    With every pebble stops to play;
Taking no note of space nor time,
    Through flowers, the banks adorning,

Still rolling on, with silver chime,
  In star-clad night and golden morning.
So went Love on, through cold and heat,
Singing, "The Daisy's ever sweet."
'Twas then the flowers were haunted
  With fairy forms and lovely things,
Whose beauty elder bards have chanted,
  And how they lived in crystal springs,
And swang upon the honied bells;
  In meadows danced round dark green mazes,
Strewed flowers around the holy wells,
  But never trampled on the Daisies.
They spared the star that lit their feet,
The Daisy was so very sweet.

Miller.

When soothed awhile by milder airs,
Thee Winter in the garland wears
That thinly shades his few gray hairs;
      Spring cannot shun thee;
Whole summer fields are thine by right,
And autumn, melancholy wight,
Doth in thy crimson head delight,
      When rains are on thee.
In shoals and bands, a morrice train,
Thou greet'st the traveller in the lane;
If welcomed once thou count'st it gain,
      Thou art not daunted;
Nor car'st if thou be set at naught:
And oft alone in nooks remote
We meet thee, like a pleasant thought,
      When such are wanted.

Wordsworth.

I cannot gaze on aught that wears
　　The beauty of the skies,
Or aught that in life's valley bears
　　The hues of paradise;
I cannot look upon a star,
Or cloud that seems a seraph's car,
Or any form of purity—
Unmingled with a dream of thee.

　　　　　　　　　P. Benjamin.

The Daisy scattered on each meade and downe,
A golden tuft within a silver crown;
Faire fell that dainty flower! and may there be
No shepherd graced that doth not honour thee.

　　　　　　　　　Browne.

There is a flower, a little flower
　　With silver crest and golden eye,
That welcomes every changing hour,
　　And weathers every sky.

　　　　　　　　　Montgomery.

Heaven may awhile correct the virtuous,
Yet it will wipe their eyes again, and make
Their faces whiter with their tears.　Innocence
Concealed is the stolen pleasure of the gods,
Which never ends in shame, as that of men
Doth oftentimes do; but like the sun breaks forth,
When it hath gratified another world;
And to our unexpecting eyes appears
More glorious through its late obscurity.

　　　　　　　　　John Fountain.

PERIWINKLE.... *Tender Recollections.*

IN France, the Periwinkle has been adopted as the emblem of the pleasures of memory and sincere friendship, probably in allusion to Rousseau's recollection of his friend, Madame de Warens, occasioned, after a lapse of thirty years, by the sight of this flower, which they together had admired. This plant is deeply rooted in the soil which it adorns. It throws out its shoots on all sides to clasp the earth, and covers it with flowers, which reflect the hue of heaven. Thus our first affections, warm, pure, and artless, seem to be of heavenly origin.

> Though the rock of my last hope is shivered,
>   And its fragments are sunk in the wave,
> Though I feel that my soul is delivered
>   To pain,—it shall not be its slave.
> There is many a pang to pursue me:
>   They may crush, but they shall not contemn;
> They may torture, but shall not subdue me,—
>   'Tis of thee that I think, not of them.
> *Byron.*

> 'Tis sweet, and yet 'tis sad, that gentle power,
> Which throws in winter's lap the spring-tide flower:
> I love to dream of days my childhood knew,
> When, with the sister of my heart, time flew
> On wings of innocence and hope! dear hours,
> When joy sprang up about our path, like flowers!
> *Mrs. A. M. Wells.*

The lesser Periwinkle's bloom,
Like carpet of Damascus' loom,
Pranks with bright blue the tissue wove
Of verdant foliage: and above
With milk-white flowers, whence soon shall swell
Red fruitage, to the taste and smell
Pleasant alike, the Strawberry weaves
Its coronets of three-fold leaves
In mazes through the sloping wood.

Mant.

Where captivates the sky-blue Periwinkle
Under the cottage eaves.

Hurdis.

Remember thee?
Yea, from the table of my memory
I'll wipe away all trivial fond records,
All saws of books, all forms, all pressures past,
That youth and observation copied there;
And thy commandment all alone shall live
Within the book and volume of my brain,
Unmixed with baser matter.

Shakspeare.

Oh! only those
Whose souls have felt this one idolatry
Can tell how precious is the slightest thing
Affection gives and hallows! A dead flower
Will long be kept, remembrancer of looks
That made each leaf a treasure.

Miss Landon.

SWEET-BRIER, OR EGLANTINE....*Poetry.*

THE Eglantine is the poet's flower. In the floral games, it was the prize for the best composition on the charms of study and eloquence. Though its flowers are most beautiful in hue, their fragrance is their more valuable quality. In like manner, the charms of poetry and eloquence should be considered superior to those of appearance.

And well the poet, at her shrine,
　　May bend and worship while he woos;
To him she is a thing divine,
The inspiration of his line,
　　His loved one, and his muse.
If to his song the echo rings
　　Of fame—'tis woman's voice he hears; ·
If ever from his lyre's proud strings
Flow sounds, like rush of angel wings,
'Tis that she listens, while he sings,
　　With blended smiles and tears.
　　　　　　　　　　　　Halleck.

Give me the poet's lyre!
And as the seraph in his orbit sings,
Oh, may I strike the heaven-attuned strings,
　　With a seraphic fire!
With music fill the mighty dome of mind,
And the rapt souls of men in music brightly bind!
　　　　　　　　　　　J. W. H.

    Trace the young poet's fate;
Fresh from his solitude, the child of dreams,
His heart upon his lips he seeks the world,
To find him fame and fortune, as if life
Were like a fairy tale. His song has led
The way before him; flatteries fill his ear,
His presence courted, and his words are caught;
And he seems happy in so many friends.
What marvel if he somewhat overrate
His talents and his state? These scenes soon change.
The vain, who sought to mix their name with his;
The curious, who but live for some new sight;
The idle—all these have been gratified,
And now neglect stings even more than scorn.

                        Miss Landon.

LILAC....*First Emotions of Love.*

THE freshness of the verdure of the Lilac; the flexibility of its branches; the profusion of its flowers; their transitory beauty and their soft hues,—all remind us of those emotions which embellish beauty, and throw such a light around our youthful hours. It is said that Van Spaendonc himself threw down his pencil on viewing a group of Lilacs. Nature seems to have delighted in creating its delicate clusters, which astonish by their beauty and variety. The fragrance of the flowers is even more gratifying than their beauty.

          She had grown,
In her unstained seclusion, bright and pure
As a first opening Lilac, when it spreads
Its clear leaves to the sweetest dawn of May.

                        Percival.

When first thou camest, gentle, shy, and fond,
　My purest, first-born love, and dearest treasure,
My heart received thee with a joy beyond
　All that it yet had felt of earthly pleasure;
Nor thought that any love again might be
So deep and strong, as that I felt for thee.
Mrs. Norton.

I love thee,—and I live!　The moon,
　Who sees me from her calm above,
The wind, who weaves her dim, soft tune
　About me, know how much I love!
Naught else, save night, and the lonely hour,
　E'er heard my passion wild and strong;
Even *thou* yet deem'st not of thy power,
　Unless thou read'st aright my song!
Barry Cornwall.

She loves—but knows not whom she loves,
　Nor what his race, nor whence he came;—
Like one who meets, in Indian groves,
　Some beauteous bird without a name,
Brought by the last ambrosial breeze,
From isles in the undiscovered seas,
To show his plumage for a day
To wondering eyes, and wing away!
Moore.

Tulip....*Declaration of Love.*

THE Tulip is an extraordinary favourite in many parts of Europe and Asia; and, in Holland and Turkey, the most extravagant prices are paid for fine specimens. On account of the elegance of its form, the beauty of its colours, and its want of fragrance and other useful qualities, this flower has been considered as an appropriate symbol of a female who possesses no recommendation but a beautiful appearance. In the East, the Tulip is employed as the emblem by which a lover makes known his passion to his mistress; as the Tulip expresses the idea that he has a face all fire and a heart all coal.

> Not one of Flora's brilliant race
>   A form more perfect can display:
> Art could not feign more simple grace,
>   Nor 'Nature take a line away.
> Yet, rich as morn, of many a hue,
>   When flushing clouds through darkness strike,
> The Tulip's petals shine in dew,
>   All beautiful, but none alike.
>
>   *Montgomery.*

> My heart is sad and lonely,
>   With weariness I pine;
> Would thou wert here, mine only,—
>   Would I were wholly thine!
>
>   *H. J. H.*

DAISY WALL FLOWER AND TULIP

Your innocence and fidelity in misfortune
have caused me to declare my love for you

If spirits, pure as those who kneel
  Around the throne of light above,
The power of beauty's spell could feel,
  And lose a heaven for woman's love,—
What marvel that a heart like mine
  Enraptured by thy charms should be!
Forget to bend at glory's shrine,
  And lose itself—ay, heaven—for thee!
                      Memorial.

Fain would I speak the thoughts I bear to thee,
But they do choke and flutter in my throat,
And make me like a child.
                    Joanna Baillie.

CYPRESS....*Mourning.*

THE ancients consecrated the Cypress to the Fates,
the Furies and Pluto. They placed it near tombs.
The people of the East retain the same custom in the
decoration of their cemeteries. The Turks plant the
Cypress at the head and at the foot of the graves.
According to Ovid, the Cypress derived its name from
Cyparissos, an especial friend of Apollo's, who, in
grief at having inadvertently killed a favourite stag of
his, prayed the gods that his mourning might be made
perpetual, and was changed into a Cypress tree, the
branches of which were thenceforward used at funerals.

      Lady dear! this history
        Is thy fated lot,
      Ever such thy watching
        For what cometh not,

4

Till with anxious waiting dull,
Round thee fades the beautiful;
Still thou seekest on, though weary,
    Seeking still in vain.

Miss Landon.

Thou art lost to me for ever,—I have lost thee, Isadore,
Thy head will never rest upon my loyal bosom more.
Thy tender eyes will never more gaze fondly into mine,
Nor thine arms around me lovingly and trustingly en-
    twine.
Thou art dead and gone, loving wife,—thy heart is
    still and cold,—
And I at one stride have become most comfortless and
    old;
Of our whole world of love and song, thou wast the
    only light,
A star, whose setting left behind, ah! me, how dark a
    night!
    Thou art lost to me, for ever, Isadore.

Albert Pike.

The Cypress is the emblem of mourning.

Shakspeare.

Alas, for earthly joy, and hope, and love,
    Thus stricken down, e'en in their holiest hour!
What deep, heart-wringing anguish must they prove,
    Who live to weep the blasted tree or flower!
Oh, wo, deep wo to earthly love's fond trust,
When all it once has worshipped lies in dust!

Mrs. Embury.

WALL-FLOWER....*Fidelity in Adversity.*

THIS flower derives its name from the circumstance of its growing upon old walls, the casements and battlements of ancient castles, and among the ruins of abbeys. The troubadors were accustomed to wearing a bouquet of Wall-flowers, as the emblem of an affection which is proof against time and the frowns of fortune.

> *Adah.*—Alas! thou sinnest now, my Cain; thy words
> Sound impious in mine ears.
>   *Cain.*—Then leave me!
>   *Adah.*—Never,
> Though thy God left thee!
>
> > > > > *Byron.*

> An emblem true thou art
>   Of love's enduring lustre given
> To cheer a lonely heart.
>
> > > > *Barton.*

> Flower of the solitary place!
>   Gray Ruin's golden crown,
> That lendest melancholy grace
>   To haunts of old renown;
> Thou mantlest o'er the battlements
>   By strife or storm decayed;
> And fillest up each envious rent
>   Time's canker-tooth hath made.
>
> > > > *Moir.*

Though human, thou didst not deceive me;
    Though woman, thou didst not forsake;
Though loved, thou forborest to grieve me;   ·
    Though slandered, thou never couldst shake;
Though trusted, thou didst not disclaim me;
    Though parted, it was not to fly;
Though watchful, 'twas not to defame me;
    Nor, mute, that the world might belie.

Byron.

Yes, love! my breast, at sorrow's call,
    Shall tremble like thine own;
If from those eyes the tear-drops fall,
    They shall not fall alone.
Our souls, like heaven's aerial bow,
Blend every light within their glow,
    Of joy or sorrow known;
And grief, divided with thy heart,
Were sweeter far than joy apart.

Anon.

HAWTHORN....*Hope.*

VARIOUS significations have been given to the Hawthorn. Among the Turks, a branch of it expresses the
wish of a lover to receive a kiss from the object of his
affection. Among the ancient Greeks, the Hawthorn
was a symbol of conjugal union; its blossomed boughs
were carried about at their wedding festivities, and the
newly-married couple were even lighted to their bridal
chamber with torches made of its wood. In England,
the Hawthorn is used in the sports of May-days,
and is, therefore, frequently called May. There is a

proverb among the rural inhabitants of that country, that a "store of haws portend cold winters." Though the Hawthorn is quoted as the emblem of Hope, it must be considered more particularly as the lover's hope.

HOW MAY WAS FIRST MADE.

As Spring upon a silver cloud
  Lay looking on the world below,
Watching the breezes as they bowed
  The buds and blossoms to and fro,
She saw the fields with Hawthorns walled:
  Said Spring, "New buds I will create."
She to a Flower-Spirit called,
  Who on the month of May did wait,
And bade her fetch a Hawthorn-spray,
That she might make the buds of May.
Said Spring, "The grass looks green and bright,
  The Hawthorn-hedges too are green,
I'll sprinkle them with flowers of light,
  Such stars as earth has never seen;
And all through England's girded vales,
  Her steep hill-sides and haunted streams,
Where woodlands dip into the dales,
  Where'er the Hawthorn stands and dreams,
Where thick-leaved trees make dark the day,
I'll light each nook with flowers of May.
Like pearly dew-drops, white and round,
  The shut-up buds shall first appear,
And in them be such fragrance found,
  As breeze before did never bear;

Such as in Eden only dwelt,
　When angels hovered round its bowers,
And long-haired Eve at morning knelt
　In innocence amid the flowers:
While the whole air was, every way,
Filled with a perfume sweet as May.
And oft shall groups of children come,
　Threading their way through shady places,
From many a peaceful English home,
　The sunshine falling on their faces;
Starting with merry voice the thrush,
　As through green lanes they wander singing,
To gather the sweet Hawthorn bush;
　Which, homeward in the evening bringing
With smiling faces, they shall say,
' There's nothing half so sweet as May.'
And many a poet yet unborn
　Shall link its name with some sweet lay,
And lovers oft at early morn
　Shall gather blossoms of the May;
With eyes bright as the silver dews,
　Which on the rounded May-buds sleep,
And lips, whose parted smiles diffuse
　A sunshine o'er the watch they keep,
Shall open all their white array
Of pearls, ranged like the buds of May."
Spring shook the cloud on which she lay,
And silvered o'er the Hawthorn spray,
Then showered down the buds of May.
　　　　　　　　　　　　　Miller.

With hope all pleases, nothing comes amiss.
　　　　　　　　　　　　　Rogers.

And Hawthorn's early blooms appear,
Like youthful hope upon life's year.

.   *Drayton.*

Gay was the love of paradise he drew
And pictured in his fancy ; he did dwell
Upon it till it had a life ; he threw
A tint of heaven athwart it—who can tell
The yearnings of his heart, the charm, the spell,
That bound him to that vision ?

                                      Percival.

LOVE-LIES-BLEEDING....*Deserted Love.*

THIS beautiful emblem of love, wounded and bereaved
by fate, is a species of Amaranthus. The flower is of
a reddish-purple hue, which circumstance suggests its
name.

A single rose is shedding
   Its lovely lustre meek and pale :
It looks as planted by despair—
   So white, so faint—the slightest gale
Might whirl the leaves on high.

                                      Byron.

And on with many a step of pain,
   Our weary race is sadly run ;
And still, as on we plod our way,
   We find, as life's gay dreams depart,
To close our being's troubled day,
   Naught left us but a broken heart.

                                      Percival.

Nor would I change my buried love
For any heart of living mould,
No—for I am a hero's child—
I'll hunt my quarry in the wild;
And still my home this mansion make,
Of all unheeded and unheeding,
And cherish, for my warrior's sake,
The flower of Love-lies-bleeding.

Campbell.

Upon her face there was the tint of grief,
The settled shadow of an inward strife,
And an unquiet drooping of the eye,
As if its lid were charged with unshed tears.

Byron.

MYRTLE....*Love.*

THE Myrtle has ever been consecrated to Venus.
At Rome, the temple of the goddess was surrounded
by a grove of Myrtles; and in Greece, she was adorned
under the name of Myrtilla. It was observed by the
ancients, that, wherever the Myrtle grew, it excluded
all other plants. So love, wherever it is permitted to
grow, excludes all other feelings. The ladies of modern
Rome retain a strong affection for this plant, preferring
its odour to that of the most fragrant essences.

Our love came as the early dew
  Comes unto drooping flowers;
Dropping its first sweet freshness on
  Our life's dull, lonely hours.

Mrs. R. S. Nichols.

Love is a celestial harmony
Of likely hearts, composed of stars' consent,
Which join together in sweet sympathy,
To work each other's joy and true content,
Which they have harboured since their first descent,
Out of their heavenly bowers, where they did see
And know each other here beloved to be.

Spenser.

I have done penance for contemning love;
Whose high imperious thoughts have punished me
With bitter fasts, with penitential groans,
With nightly tears, and daily heart-sore sighs.

Shakspeare.

The Myrtle on thy breast or brow
Would lively hope and love avow.

J. H. Wiffen.

Comfort cannot soothe
The heart whose life is centred in the thought
Of happy loves, once known, and still in hope,
Living with a consuming energy.

Percival.

As in the sweetest bud
The eating canker dwells, so eating love
Inhabits in the finest wits of all.

Shakspeare.

LILY OF THE VALLEY....*Modesty.*

THE beautiful Lily of the Valley is the fit emblem of the union of beauty, simplicity, and love of retirement. It adds an indescribable charm to the spots where it blooms. Its snowy hues and general delicacy of appearance excite emotions of a kindred nature to those we experience in the company of one whose heart is free from guile, and whose manners are gentle and unpretending.

> Lilacs then, and daffodillies,
> And the nice-leaved, lesser Lilies,
> Shading, like detected light,
> Their little green-tipt lamps of white.
>
> *Hunt.*

> I had found out a sweet green spot,
>   Where a Lily was blooming fair;
> The din of the city disturbed it not,
> But the spirit that shades the quiet cot
>   With its wings of love was there.
> I found that Lily's bloom,
>   When the day was dark and chill;
> It smiled like a star in a misty gloom,
> And it sent abroad a soft perfume,
>   Which is floating around me still.
>
> *Percival.*

> The Lily, in whose snow-white bells
> Simplicity delights and dwells.
>
> *Balfour.*

HYACINTH....*Constancy.*

THE blue Hyacinth is mentioned by several English writers as the emblem of constancy. There are many varieties found in Europe and America, but the variety known in Scotland as the "Blue Bell" is the most common and the most celebrated.

When daisies blush, and wind-flowers wet with dew,
When shady lanes with Hyacinth's are blue,
When the elm blossoms o'er the brooding bird,
And, wild and wide, the plover's wail is heard,
Where melts the mist on mountains far away,
Till morn is kindled into brightest day.

Elliott.

Then come the wild weather, come sleet, or come snow,
We will stand by each other however it blow.
Oppression and sickness, and sorrow, and pain,
Shall be to our true love as links to the chain.

Longfellow.

She loves him yet!
The flower the false one gave her
When last he came,
Is still with her wild tears wet.
She'll ne'er forget,
Howe'er his faith may waver,
Through grief and shame,
Believe it,—she loves him yet!

Mrs. Osgood.

Over the moorland, over the lea,
Dancing airily, there are we:
Sometimes, mounted on stems aloft,
　We wave o'er broom and heather,
To meet the kiss of the zephyr soft;
　Sometimes, close together,
Tired of dancing, tired of peeping,
Under the whin you'll find us sleeping.
Daintily bend we our honied bells,
While the gossipping bee her story tells,
And drowsily hums and murmurs on
Of the wealth to her waxen storehouse gone;
And though she gathers our sweets the while,
We welcome her in with a nod and a smile.
No rock is too high—no vale too low,
For our fragile and tremulous forms to grow.
　　Sometimes we crown
The castle's dizziest tower, and look
　　Laughingly down
On the pigmy men in the world below,
　Wearily wandering to and fro.
Sometimes we dwell on the cragged crest　·
　　Of mountain high,
And the ruddy sun, from the blue sea's breast,
　　Climbing the sky,
Looks from his couch of glory up,
And lights the dew in the bluebell's cup.
We are crowning the mountain
　　With azure bells,
　Or decking the fountains
　　In forest dells,
Or wreathing the ruin with clusters gray,

And nodding and laughing the livelong day;   ·
Then chiming our lullaby, tired with play.
Are we not beautiful?   Oh! are not we
The darlings of mountain and moorland and lea?
Plunge in the forest—are we not fair?
Go to the high-road—we'll meet ye there.
Oh! where is the flower that content may tell,
Like the laughing and nodding and dancing bluebell.

Louisa A. Twamley.

The Hyacinth's for constancy,
Wi' its unchanging blue.

Burns.

ORCHIS.....*A Belle.*

THE Butterfly Orchis is rather rare except where
there is a chalky soil. The Spider Orchis has gained
its name from the great resemblance it bears to one of
those large, fat-bodied garden spiders, which are often
noticed for the singular beauty of the markings on
their backs. Another is so very like a fly, that it is
named the Fly Orchis; another is like a lizard, or
some strange reptile, and the flowers being yellow,
green, and purple, and twisted in and about one another in a very odd way, it really looks like some horrible group of queer living creatures. One, from being
fancied like a man, is called Man Orchis; another,
very gayly spotted, and ornamented with a helmet-like

appendage, is the Military Orchis; another is called
Bee Orchis. Bishop Mant thus alludes to some of
these:

> Well boots it the thick-mantled leas
> To traverse: if boon nature grant,
> To crop the insect-seeming plant,
> The vegetable Bee; or nigh
> Of kin, the long-horned Butterfly,
> White, or his brother purple pale,
> Scenting alike the evening gale;
> The Satyr flower, the pride of Kent,
> Of Lizard form, and goat-like scent.

No wonder that cheek in its beauty transcendent,
  Excelleth the beauty of others by far;
No wonder that eye is so richly resplendent,
  For your heart is a rose and your soul is a star.

Mrs. Osgood.

What right have you, madam, gazing in your shining
    mirror daily,
Getting so by heart your beauty, which all others must
    adore;
While you draw the golden ringlets down your fingers,
    to vow gayly,
You will wed no man that's only good to God,—and
    nothing more.

Miss Barrett.

Box.....*Stoicism.*

THE common Box, of which our hedge is formed, is indigenous in England, preferring the chalky hills of Surrey and Kent for its residence, but flourishing well on other soils. It is one of the most useful evergreen shrubs we possess, and especially as it will grow under the drip and shadow of other trees, as you know is the case with our hedge. It is found in most European countries, from Britain southwards, also about Mount Caucasus, Persia, China, Cochin China, and America. It was formerly much more common in England than now, having disappeared under the spread of agriculture. Box-hill, in Surrey, is named from this tree, and is a conical elevation covered with a wood of Box-trees, some of large size. Boxley in Kent, and Boxwell in Gloucestershire, are also named from it. The leaf and general appearance of the tree are too familiar to require any description. The scent of the spring blossoms is rather powerful, and to some persons unpleasant. The timber is very valuable, it is sold by weight, and, being very hard and smooth, and not apt to warp, is well adapted for many nice and delicate purposes. In the days of good old Evelyn, it appears to have been as much used as at present, for he says, "It is good for the turner, engraver, carver, mathematical instrument maker, comb and pipe, or flute-maker, and the roots for the inlayer and cabinet-maker. Of box are made wheels, sheaves, pins, pegs for musical instruments, nut-crackers, button-moulds, weavers' shuttles, hollar-sticks, bump-sticks, and dressers for the shoemaker, rulers, rolling-pins, pestles, mall-balls, beetles, tops, chessmen, tables, screws, bobbins for bone-lace, spoons, knife-handles, but especially combs." Most of those engravings in books, called wood-cuts, are done upon Box wood, and for that purpose English Box is superior to any other, though a great portion of what is used in this country comes from the Levant. The ancients used combs made of Box-wood, and also instruments to be played on with the mouth. The Romans used to adorn their gardens with it, clipped into form, as we find from mention being made of clipped Box-trees by their writers. It was formerly much cut in this manner here, and was ranked next to the Yew for its capabilities of taking artificial and grotesque forms; but except a few ancient hedges of Box, like our own, and those at Castle Bromwich Hall, where the Yew hedges are also preserved, there are not many vestiges of its former garden-glory remaining. A dwarf kind is used for making a neat and firm edging to flower borders, for which nothing answers so well, or produces so proper an effect.

> Though youth be past, and beauty fled,
>   The constant heart its pledge redeems,
> Like Box, that guards the flowerless bed,
>   And brighter from the contrast seems.
>   *Mrs. Hale.*

NARCISSUS AND DAFFODIL....*Self-Love.*

THERE are several species of the Narcissus. The
Yellow Narcissus is better known as the Daffodil, and
bears much resemblance to the Yellow Lily. The
Poetic Narcissus is the largest of the species, and may
be distinguished by the crimson border of the very
shallow and almost flat cup of the nectary. Shakspeare, in his Winter's Tale, speaks of

Daffodils,
That come before the swallow dares, and taste
The winds of March with beauty.

The ancients attributed the origin of the Narcissus to
the metamorphosis of a beautiful youth of that name,
who, having slighted the love of the nymph Echo, became enamoured of his own image, which he beheld in
a fountain, and pined to death in consequence.

I wandered lonely, as a cloud
  That floats on high o'er vales and hills
When all at once I saw a crowd,
  A host of golden Daffodils;
Beside the lake, beneath the trees,
Fluttering and dancing in the breeze.
Continuous as the stars that shine
  And twinkle on the milky way,
They stretched in never-ending line
  Along the margin of the bay;
Ten thousand saw I at a glance,
Tossing their heads in sprightly dance.

5

The waves beside them danced, but they
   Outdid the sparkling waves in glee;
A poet could not but be gay
   In such a joyful company:
I gazed—and gazed—but little thought
What wealth to me the show had brought.
For oft when on my couch I lie,
   In vacant or in pensive mood,
They flash upon that inward eye
   Which is the bliss of solitude.
And then my heart with pleasure fills,
And dances with the Daffodils.
              Wordsworth.

Nature's laws must be obeyed,
And this is one she strictly laid
On every soul which she has made,
   Down from our earliest mother:
Be *self* your first and greatest care,
From all reproach the darling spare,
And any blame that she should bear,
   Put off upon another.
              Miss Gould.

     The pale Narcissus
Still feeds upon itself; but, newly blown,
The nymphs will pluck it from its tender stalk,
And say, "Go, fool, and to thy image talk."
              Lord Thurlow.

LILY....*Majesty.*

THE Lily's height and beauty speak command. The Jews imitated its form in the decorations of their first magnificent temple; and Christ described it as more splendid than King Solomon in his most gorgeous apparel. According to ancient mythology, there was originally but one species of Lily, and that was orange-coloured; and the white was produced by the following circumstance:—Jupiter, wishing to render Hercules immortal, prevailed on Juno to take a deep draught of nectar, which threw the queen into a profound sleep. Jupiter then placed the infant Hercules at her breast, so that the divine milk might ensure immortality. Hercules drew the milk faster than he could swallow it, and some drops fell to the earth, from which immediately sprang the White Lily.

> Flowers of the fairest,
> And gems of the rarest,
> I find and I gather in country or town;
> But one is still wanting,
> Oh! where is it haunting?
> The bud and the jewel must make up my crown.
> Thou pearl of the deep sea
> That flows in my heart free,
> Thou rock-planted Lily, come hither, or send;
> Mid flowers of the fairest,
> And gems of the rarest,
> I miss thee, I seek thee, my own parted friend!
>
> *M. J. Jewsbury.*

Ye well arrayed———
Queen Lilies—and ye painted populace,
Who dwell in fields, and lead ambrosial lives.

Young.

The wand-like Lily, which lifted up,
As a Mœnad, its radiant-coloured cup,
Till the fiery star, which is in its eye,
Gazed through clear dew on the tender sky.

Shelley.

Her glossy hair is clustered o'er a brow
  Bright with intelligence, and fair and smooth;
Her eyebrow's shape is like the aerial bow,
  Her cheek all purple with the beam of youth,
Mounting at times to a transparent glow,
  As if her veins ran lightning; she, in sooth,
Has a proud air, and grace by no means common,
Her stature tall,—I hate a dumpy woman.

Byron.

Oh, he is all made up of love and charms,
Whatever maid could wish or man admire;
Delight of every eye! when he appears,
A secret pleasure gladdens all that see him;
And when he talks, the proudest men will blush
To hear his virtues and his glory!

Addison.

Moss Rose.... *Confession of Love.*

THE origin of this exquisitely beautiful variety of the
Rose is thus fancifully accounted for:—

> The Angel of the Flowers one day,
> Beneath a Rose-tree sleeping lay,
> That spirit to whose charge is given
> To bathe young buds in dews from heaven.
> Awaking from his light repose,
> The angel whispered to the Rose,
> "O fondest object of my care,
> Still fairest found where all are fair,
> For the sweet shade thou hast given to me,
> Ask what thou wilt, 'tis granted thee."
> Then said the Rose, with deepening glow,
> "On me another grace bestow."
> The spirit paused in silent thought—
> What grace was there that flower had not?
> 'Twas but a moment—o'er the Rose
> A veil of moss the angel throws;
> And, robed in nature's simplest weed,
> Could there a flower that Rose exceed?
>
> *Anon.*

> They gather gems with sunbeams bright,
>   From floating clouds and falling showers;
> They rob Aurora's locks of light,
>   To grace their own fair queen of flowers.
> Thus, thus adorned, the speaking rose
>   Becomes a *token* fit to tell

Of things that words can ne'er disclose,
And naught but this reveal so well.
Then take my flower, and let its leaves
Beside thy heart be cherished near,
While that confiding heart receives
The thought it whispers to thine ear.

Token, 1830.

WHITE WATER-LILY....*Purity.*

THE White Water-Lily is the Queen of the Waves,
and reigns sole sovereign over the streams; and it was
a species of Water-Lily which the old Egyptians and
ancient Indians worshipped—the most beautiful object
that was held sacred in their superstitious creed, and
one which we cannot look upon even now without feeling a delight mingled with reverence. No flower looks
more lovely than this "Lady of the Lake," resting her
crowned head on a green throne of velvet, and looking
down into the depths of her own sky-reflecting realms,
watching the dance, as her attendant water-nymphs
keep time to the rocking of the ripples, and the dreamy
swaying of the trailing water streams.

Miller.

Thine is a face to look upon and pray
That a pure spirit keep thee—I would meet
With one so gentle by the streams away,
Living with nature; keeping thy pure feet
For the unfingered moss, and for the grass
Which leaneth where the gentle waters pass.

The autumn leaves should sigh thee to thy sleep;
And the capricious April, coming on,
Awake thee like a flower; and stars should keep
A vigil o'er thee like Endymion;
And thou for very gentleness shouldst weep
As dews of the night's quietness come down.

Willis.

Oh, come to the river's rim, come with us there,
For the White Water-Lily is wondrous fair,
With her large broad leaves on the stream afloat,
Each one a capacious fairy-boat.
The swan among flowers!   How stately ride
Her snow-white leaves on the glittering tide!
And the Dragon-fly gallantly stays to sip
A kiss of dew from her goblet's lip.

Anon.

The Lily on the water sleeping,
  Enwreathed with pearl, and bossed with gold,
    An emblem is, my love, of thee:
But when she like a nymph is peeping,
  To watch her sister-buds unfold,
    White shouldered on the flowery lea,
  Gazing about in sweet amazement,
  Thy image, from the vine-clad casement,
    Seems looking out, my love, on me.

Miller.

Little streams have flowers a many,
Beautiful and fair as any;
Typha strong, and green bur reed,
Willow herb with cotton seed,

Arrow head with eye of jet,
And the Water-Violet;
There the flowering Rush you meet,
And the plumy meadow sweet,
And in places deep and stilly
Marble-like, the Water-Lily.

Mrs. Howitt.

MARIGOLD....*Grief.*

THE Marigold is the conventional emblem of distress
of mind. It is distinguished by many singular properties. It blossoms the whole year, and on that account, the Romans termed it the flower of the calends,
or of all the months. Its flowers are open only from
nine in the morning till three in the afternoon. They
always follow the course of the sun, by turning from
east to west as he proceeds upon his daily journey.
In July and August these flowers emit, during the
night, small luminous sparks. Alone, the Marigold
expresses grief; interwoven with other flowers, the
varied events of life; the cloud and sunshine of ill and
good.

And see the flaunting Marigold,
Gay from its marshy bed unfold
Mid minor lights its disks that shine
Like suns for brightness.

Anon.

Open afresh your round of starry folds,
Ye ardent Marigolds!
Dry up the moisture of your golden lids.

Keats.

When, with a serious musing, I behold
The grateful and obsequious Marigold,
How duly, every morning, she displays
Her open breast when Phœbus spreads his rays;
How she observes him in his daily walk
Still bending towards him her small slender stalk;
How, when he down declines, she droops and mourns,
Bedewed as 'twere with tears till he returns.
                                        Withers.

I need not say how, one by one,
    Love's flowers have dropped from off love's chain,
Enough to say that they are gone,
    And that they cannot bloom again.
                                        Miss Landon.

We sometimes see a shadow swiftly skim
    In summer o'er the hills and vales of earth:
    So transient shades steal o'er the face of mirth,
And frequent tears the brightest eyes bedim.
                                        MacKellar.

Thine is a grief that wastes the heart,
    Like mildew on a tulip's dyes—
When hope, deferred but to depart,
    Loses its smiles but keeps its sighs.
                                        Miss Landon.

WHITE ROSE....*I would be single.*

How uneasy is his life
Who is troubled with a wife!
Be she ne'er so fair or comely,
Be she foul or be she homely,
Be she blithe or melancholy,
Have she wit, or have she folly,
Be she prudent, be she squandering,
Be she staid, or be she wandering,
Yet uneasy is his life
Who is married to a wife.

Cotton.

THE White Rose became celebrated in English history as the badge of the house of York, in the War of the Roses. Among the ancients, who considered the Rose as the queen of flowers, it was the custom to crown new-married persons with a chaplet of Red and White Roses; and in the procession of the Corybantes, the goddess Cybele, the protectress of cities, was pelted with White Roses.

A single Rose is shedding
Its lovely lustre meek and pale:
It looks as planted by despair—
So white, so faint—the slightest gale
Might whirl the leaves on high.

Byron.

YELLOW ROSE....*Jealousy.*

PFEFFEL, a German poet, has pleasingly accounted
for the origin of the Yellow Rose, the emblem of envy
and jealousy, in the following manner:

Once a White Rose-bud reared her head,
And peevishly to Flora said,
"Look at my sister's blushing hue—
Pray, mother, let me have it too."
"Nay, child," was Flora's mild reply,
"Be thankful for such gifts as I
Have deemed befitting to dispense—
Thy dower the hue of innocence."
When did Persuasion's voice impart
Content and peace to female heart
Where baleful Jealousy bears sway,
And scares each gentler guest away?
The Rose still grumbled and complained,
Her mother's bounties still disdained.
"Well, then," said angered Flora—"take"—
She breathed upon her as she spake—
"Henceforth no more in simple vest
Of innocence shalt thou be drest—
Take that which better suits thy mind,
The hue for Jealousy designed!"
The Yellow Rose has from that hour
Borne evidence of Envy's power.

                Is whispering nothing?
Is leaning cheek to cheek?—is meeting noses?
Kissing with inside lip?—stopping the career
Of laughter with a sigh?—(a note infallible
Of breaking honesty:)—horsing foot to foot?—
Skulking in corners?—wishing clocks more swift?—
Hours, minutes?—noon, midnight? and all eyes
Blind with the pin and web, but theirs,—theirs only,.
That would unseen be wicked?—is this nothing?
Why, then the world, and all that's in it, is nothing.
                          Shakspeare.

Thou wondrous yellow fiend!
Temper an antidote with antimony,
And 'tis infectious: Mix jealousy with marriage, .
It poisons virtue.
                          Davenport.

O jealousy! thou bane of pleasing friendship,
Thou worst invader of our tender bosoms;
How does thy rancour poison all our softness,
And turn our gentle natures into bitterness!
                          Rowe.

Ah! poor unconscious rival maid,
How drearily must thou sicken and fade, ·
'Neath jealousy's dark Upas shade!
                          Tupper.

RED ROSE.....*Beauty and Love.*

ACCORDING to ancient fable, the red colour of the Rose may be traced to Venus, whose delicate foot, when she was hastening to the relief of her beloved Adonis, was pierced by a thorn that drew blood,

> Which on the White Rose being shed,
> Made it for ever after red.
>
> *Herrick.*

Miller, the "basket-maker" and poet, gives the following beautiful account of the origin of the Red Rose :—

It was drawing toward the decline of a beautiful summer day, when the red, round sun was bending down a deep, blue, unclouded sky, to where a vast range of mountains stretched, summit upon summit, and in the far distance again rose, pile upon pile, until high over all towered the god-haunted height of cloud-capt Olympus, rising with its rounded shoulder, like another world, on the uttermost rim of the horizon. At the foot of this immense world of untrodden mountains, opened out a wide, immeasurable forest, stretching far away, league upon league, with its unexplored ocean of trees, which were bounded somewhere by another range of unknown mountains, that again overlooked a vast, silent, and unpeopled world. On the edge of this pathless desert of trees, and nearest the foot of Olympus, sat the Queen of Beauty and of Love; with her golden tresses unbound, and her matchless countenance buried within the palms of her milk-white hands, and sobbing as if her fond, immortal heart would break. Beside her was laid the dead body of Adonis, his face half-hidden beneath the floating fall of her hair, as she bent over him and wept. Beyond them lay the stiffened bulk of the grim and grisly boar, his hideous jaws flecked with blood and foam, and his terrible tusks glittering like the heads of pointed spears, as they stood out, sharp and white, in the unclouded sunset. Not an immortal comforter was by: for the far-seeing eye of Jove was fixed listlessly upon the golden nectar-cup, as it passed from hand to hand, along the rounded circle of the gods, while they were recounting the deeds of other days, when they waged war against the Titans. Even the chariot of Venus stood unyoked at the foot of the mount; the silken traces lay loosely thrown together upon the ground, and the white doves were idly hovering round in the air; for the weeping goddess was so overwhelmed with sorrow, that she had forgotten to waft her light-winged whisper to the Mount of Olympus; nor had they received any summons from the charioteer Love, who lay sleeping upon a bed of Roses, with his bow and arrows by his side.

In the glade of this vast forest of the old primeval world, whose echoes had never been startled by the blows of a descending axe, nor a branch rent from their majestic boles, saving by the dreaded bolts of the Thunderer, or some earth-shaking storm, which, in his anger, he had blown abroad, the Goddess of Beauty still continued to sit, as if unconscious of the savage solitude which surrounded her; nor did she notice the back-kneed Satyrs, that peered upon her unrobed loveliness with burning eyes, from many a shadowy recess in the thick-leaved underwood. Upon the trunks of the mighty and storm-tortured trees, the sunset here and there flashed down in rays of molten gold, making their gnarled and twisted stems look as if they had just issued red-hot from the jaws of some cavern-like furnace, whose glare the fancy might still trace in a blackened avenue of trees, up which the red ranks of the consuming lightning had ages agone marched. Every way, where the lengthened shadows of evening began to fall in deeper masses, the forest assumed a more savage look, which was heightened by the noise of some deadly-tusked boar, as he went snorting and thundering through the thicket; the growl of the tiger was also heard at intervals, as he retreated farther into the deepening darkness of the dingles, mistaking the blazing sunset for some devouring fire. But the eyes of Venus saw only the pale face of her lover, —she felt only his chilly and stiffened hand sink colder and deeper into the warm heart on which she pressed it, and over which her tears fell, slower or faster, just as the mournful gusts of her sorrow arose or subsided, and sent the blinding rain from the blue-veined lids that overhung her clouded eyes; for never had her immortal heart before been swollen by such an overflowing torrent of grief. But the warmth of her kisses, which would almost have awakened life in a statue of marble, fell upon lips now cold as a wintry grave; and her sighs, which came sweeter than the morning

air when it first arises from its sleep among the Roses,
stirred not one of the clotted ringlets which softened
into the yielding whiteness of her heavenly bosom,—

> "She looked upon his lips, and they are pale;
>   She took him by the hand, and that was cold;
> She whispered in his ear a heavy tale,
>   As if they heard the woful words she told."

She would have given her immortality but to have
heard those lips murmur and complain, as they had
done a few hours before—to have seen those eyes again
burning with disdain, as they flashed back indignantly
the warm advances of her love. She pictured him as
he had that very morning stood, in all the pride of
youthful manliness and beauty, when he looked down,
blushing and abashed, as he held his boar-spear in his
hand, when she threw the studded bridle over her own
rounded and naked arm, and the proud courser pricked
up his ears with delight, and shook his braided mane,
while his long tail streamed out like a banner, and
his proud eye dilated, and his broad nostrils expanded,
as he went trampling haughtily on, proud to be led
by the Queen of Beauty and of Love. She pictured
the Primrose bank on which he lay twined reluctantly
in her arms, how he tried to conceal his face, this way,
and that way, among the flowers, whenever she attempted to press his lips,—

> "While on each cheek appeared a pretty dimple:
>   Love made those hollows, if himself were slain,
> He might be buried in a tomb so simple."

She recalled his attitude as he untwined himself from
her embrace, and hurried off in pursuit of his steed,
which had snapped the rein that secured it to the
branch of a neighbouring oak, and started at full speed
down one of the wild avenues of the forest. In fancy
she again saw him, as he sat panting upon the ground,
weary with the fruitless pursuit; and how, kneeling
down, she then

> "Took him gently by the hand,
> A lily prisoned in a jail of snow,
> Or ivory in an alabaster band:
> So white a friend engirt so white a foe;
> A beauteous combat, wilful and unwilling,
> Showed like two silver doves that sat a-billing."

And as she looked upon him, she imagined that his
lips moved again, as when they said, "Give me my
hand, why dost thou feel it?" she fancied she again
felt his face upon her cheek—his kisses upon her lips,
as when she fell down and feigned herself dead; the
while he bent her fingers, and felt her pulse, and en-
deavoured by a hundred endearments and tender ex-
pressions, to restore her. And how, when she pretended
to recover, she paid him back again with unnumbered
kisses, whilst he, wearied with opposing her, no longer
offered any resistance; and how, at last, he broke from
her fair arms, and, darting down the "dark lawn," left
her seated alone upon the ground.

As picture after picture rose before her of what had
been, and every close pressure of the cold, inanimate,
but still dearly-loved form, told her what the hand of

death had done, and that those very "hopes and fears which are akin to love" were now for ever darkened and extinguished; she burst forth into such a loud, wailing lamentation, that the sound found its way unto Olympus, and fell upon the ever-open ear of Jove, who, in a moment, dashed the golden nectar-cup upon the ground, which he was about uplifting to his lips, and sprang upon his feet. There was a sound of hurrying to and fro over the mountain-summits, which sloped down to the edge of the forest—of gods and goddesses passing through the air—of golden chariots, that went whistling along like the wind, as they cleft their rapid way—and the flapping of dark, immortal wings, between which many a beautiful divinity was seated. The golden clouds of sunset gathered red and ominously about the rounded summit of Olympus, and a blood-red light glared upon such parts of the forest as were not darkened by the deepening shadows of the approaching twilight,—for the Thunderer had stamped his immortal foot, and jarred the mighty mountain to its very base. And now, in that forest glade, which but a few moments before was so wild and desolate,—where only the forms of the grisly boar, the dead Adonis, and the weeping Goddess of Beauty broke the level lines of the angry sunset, were assembled the stern Gods, and the weeping Graces, and the fluttering Loves that ever hover around the chariot of Venus. With bleeding feet and drooping head,—wan, and cold, and speechless,—was the Goddess of Beauty lifted into her golden chariot, and, with the dead body of Adonis, wafted by her silver and silent-winged doves to Mount Olympus. And then a deep darkness settled down upon the forest. When the next morning's sun arose and gilded those silent glades, the Roses, on which the blood of the Goddess of Beauty had fallen, and which were ever before white, were changed into a delicate crimson; and wherever a tear had fallen, there had sprung up a flower which the earth had never before borne, and that was the Lily of the Valley; and wherever a ruddy drop had fallen from the death-wound of Adonis sprang up the red flower which still beareth his name. Even the white apple-blossoms, which he clutched in his agony, ever after wore the ruddy stain which they caught from his folded fingers; and the drowsy Poppy grew up everywhere around the spot, as if to denote that the only consolation which can be found for sorrow is the long, unbroken sleep of death. Thus the Rose, which was before white, became red, and was ever after dedicated to Beauty and Love.

Its beautiful tint is traced to another source by a modern poet:

As erst in Eden's blissful bowers,
Young Eve surveyed her countless flowers,
An opening Rose of purest white
She marked with eye that beamed delight,
Its leaves she kissed, and straight it drew
From beauty's lip the vermeil hue.

Carey.

The poets have not exaggerated the beauty of the red-hued Rose. She would be crowned Queen of the

Flowers by the most unpoetical. The emblem of all
ages, the interpreter of all our feelings, the Rose mingles with our festivities, our joys, and our griefs. Its
fragrance is as delightful as its hues; and no truer emblem of love and beauty could have been chosen.

I have cherished

A love for one whose beauty would have charmed
In Athens. And I know what 'tis to love
A spiritual beauty, and behind the foil
Of an unblemished loveliness, still find
Charms of a higher order, and a power
Deeper and more resistless. Had I found
Such thoughts and feelings, such a clear deep stream
Of mind in one whom vulgar men had thrown
As a dull pebble from them, I had loved
Not with a love less fond, nor with a flame
Of less devotion.

Percival.

There's no miniature

In her face, but is a copious theme,
Which would, discoursed at large of, make a volume.
What clear arched brows! what sparkling eyes! the lilies
Contending with the roses in her cheeks,
Who shall most set them off. What ruby lips!—
Or unto what can I compare her neck,
But to a rock of crystal? Every limb
Proportioned to love's wish, and in their neatness
Add lustre to the richness of her habit,
Not borrowed from it.

Massinger,

PEONY....*Anger.*

THE Peony is chosen as the emblem of Anger from its red and fiery hues. It is a large double flower, and presents a superb appearance; but is almost destitute of scent.

I am burned up with inflaming wrath;
A rage, whose heat hath this condition,
That nothing can allay, nothing but blood,
The blood, and dearest valued blood, of France.
Shakspeare.

The wildest ills that darken life
Are rapture to the bosom's strife;
The tempest, in its blackest form,
Is beauty to the bosom's storm;
The ocean, lashed to fury loud,
Its high wave mingling with the cloud,
Is peaceful, sweet serenity,
To anger's dark and stormy sea.
J. W. Eastburne.

Oh, that my tongue were in the thunder's mouth!
Then with a passion would I shake the world.
Shakspeare.

NETTLES.... *Cruelty.*

NETTLES may be considered the appropriate emblem
of cruelty. How often, while in search of flowers,
have we felt the sting of these unrelenting plants!
We call that punishment cruel which visits us without
our doing an injury which deserves it; and, as we
never wished to be in the vicinity of the Nettles, nor,
therefore, to injure them, our boyish fancy looked upon
them as cruel.

> Spare not the babe,
> Whose dimpled smiles from fools exhaust their mercy;
> Think it a bastard, whom the oracle
> Hath doubtfully pronounced thy throat shall cut,
> And mince it sans remorse.
> *Shakspeare.*

> Do not insult calamity;
> It is a barbarous grossness to lay on
> The weight of scorn, where heavy misery
> Too much already weighs men's fortunes down.
> *Daniel.*

> Oh, he's accurst from all that's good,
>   Who never knew Love's healing power;
> Such sinner on his sins must brood,
>   And wait alone his hour.
> If stranger to earth's beauty—human love,
> There is no rest below, nor hope above.
> *Dana.*

COLUMBINE....*Desertion.*

BRING Lilies for a maiden's grave,
　　Roses to deck the bride,
Tulips for all who love through life
　　In brave attire to ride:
Bring each for each, in bower and hall,
But cull the Columbine for all.

"The Columbine? full many a flower
　　Hath hues more clear and bright,
Although she doth in purple go,
　　In crimson, pink, and white.
Why, when so many fairer shine,
Why choose the homely Columbine?"

Examine well each floweret's form,—
　　Read ye not something more
Than curl of petal—depth of tint?
　　Saw ye ne'er aught before
That claims a fancied semblance there.
Amid those modelled leaves so fair?

Know ye the cap which Folly wears
　　In ancient masques and plays?
Does not the Columbine recall
　　That toy of olden days?
And is not folly reigning now
O'er many a wisdom-written brow?

'Tis Folly's flower, that homely one;
   That universal guest
Makes every garden but a type
   Of every human breast;
For though ye tend both mind and bower,
There's still a nook for Folly's flower.

Then gather roses for the bride,
   Twine them in her bright hair,
But, ere the wreath be done—oh! let
   The Columbine be there.
For rest ye sure that follies dwell
In many a heart that loveth well.

Gather ye laurels for the brow
   Of every prince of song!
, For all, to whom philosophy
   And wisdom do belong.
But ne'er forget to intertwine
A flower or two of Columbine.

Forget it not;—for even they,
   The oracles of earth,
Mid all their wealth of golden thoughts,
   Their wisdom and their worth,
Sometimes play pranks beneath the sky,
Would scarce become e'en such as I!

Weave ye an armful of that plant,
   Choosing the darkest flowers,
With that red, blood-dipped wreath ye bring
   The devastating powers

Of warrior, conqueror, or chief;
Oh! twine that full of Folly's leaf!

And do ye ask me why this flower
   Is fit for every brow?
Tell me but one where Folly ne'er
   Hath dwelt, nor dwelleth now,
And I will then the laurel twine,
Unmingled with the Columbine.
Louisa A. Twamley.

PASSION FLOWER....*Faith.*

In the Passion Flower, we find a representation of
the crown of thorns, the scourge, the cross, the sponge,
the nails, and the five wounds of Christ. Hence its
name and signification.

   One more plant——
Which, consecrate to Salem's peaceful King,
Though fair as any gracing beauty's bower,
Is linked to sorrow like a holy thing,
And takes its name from suffering's fiercest hour.
Be this my noblest theme—Imperial Passion Flower!
Whatever impulse first conferred that name,
Or Fancy's dream, or Superstition's art,
I freely own its spirit-touching claim,
With thoughts and feelings it may well impart.
Barton.

Faith builds a bridge across the gulf of death,
To break the shock blind nature cannot shun,
And lands thought smoothly on the further shore.

Young.

True faith nor biddeth nor abideth form.
The bended knee, the eye uplift is all
Which man need render; all which God can bear.
What to the faith are forms? A passing speck,
A crow upon the sky.

Bailey.

Faith is the subtle chain
That binds us to the Infinite: the voice
Of a deep life within, that will remain
Until we crowd it thence.

Mrs. E. Oakes Smith.

Naught shall prevail against us, or disturb
Our cheerful faith, that all which we behold
Is full of blessings.

Wordsworth.

Ah, no! my dying lips shall close,
    Unaltered love, as faith professing;
Nor (praising Him who life bestows)
    Forget who makes that life a blessing.
My last address to Heaven is due;—
My last but one I give to you.

Lovibond.

PINK....*Pure Love.*

THE primitive Pink is simple red or white, and scented; but cultivation has varied the colour from the darkest purple to the purest white. Under all its diversities, however, it retains its delicious, spicy fragrance, and hence has been made the emblem of woman's love, which no circumstance can change. Florists designate two principal divisions of these flowers, Pinks and Carnation. The former are marked by a spot resembling an eye, and by a more humble growth. The flower of the Carnation is much larger than that of the Pink, and of a deeper hue. The Carnation was called by some of the old English writers the clove-gilly flower, from its perfume resembling that of cloves.

> She never told her love,
> But let concealment, like a worm i' the bud,
> Feed on her damask cheek; she pined in thought;
> And with a green and yellow melancholy,
> She sat (like Patience on a monument)
> Smiling at grief.
> *Shakspeare.*

> It is a fearful thing,
> To love as I love thee; to feel the world—
> The bright, the beautiful, joy giving world—
> A blank without thee. Never more to me

Can hope, joy, fear, wear different seeming. Now
I have no hope that does not dream for thee;
I have no joy that is not shared by thee;
I have no fear that does not dread for thee.

L. E. L.

Alas! the love of woman! it is known
To be a lovely and a fearful thing;
For all of theirs upon that die is thrown,
And, if 'tis lost, life has no more to bring
To them but mockeries of the past alone.

Byron.

SENSITIVE PLANT.... *Chastity.*

THIS singular plant is so named from its motions
imitating the sensibility of animal life. It contracts
itself in the evening and expands with the morning
light, and shrinks from external violence, folding up
its leaves at the mere approach of one's hand. The
Violet is the emblem of that retiring modesty which
proceeds from reflection, but the Sensitive Plant is a
perfect image of innocence and virgin modesty, the
result of instinct.

So dear to heaven is saintly chastity,
That when a soul is found sincerely so,
A thousand liveried angels lackey her,
Driving far off each thing of sin and guilt.

Milton.

Oh! she is colder than the mountain's snow.
To such a subtile purity she's wrought,
She's prayed and fasted to a walking thought:
She's an enchanted feast, most fair to sight,
And starves the appetite she does invite;
Flies from the touch of sense, and if you dare
To name but love she vanishes to air.

Crown.

In thy fair brow there's such a legend writ
Of chastity, as blinds the adulterous eye:
Not the mountain ice,
Congealed to crystals, is so frosty chaste
As thy victorious soul, which conquers man,
And man's proud tyrant-passion.

Dryden.

Like the Mimosa shrinking from
   The blight of some familiar finger—
Like flowers which but in secret bloom,
   Where aye the sheltered shadows linger,
And which beneath the hot noon-ray
Would fold their leaves and fade away—
The flowers of Love in secret cherished,
In loneliness and silence nourished,
   Shrink backward from the searching eye,
Until the stem whereon they flourished,
Their shrine, the human heart, has perished,
   Although themselves may never die.

J. G. Whittier.

Thyme....*Activity*.

Among the ancient Greeks, Thyme denoted the graceful elegance of the Attic style; because it covered Mount Hymettus, and gave an aromatic flavour to the honey made there. Those writers who had mastered the Attic style were said "to smell of Thyme." Flies of all shapes, beetles of all hues, bright butterflies, and vigilant bees for ever surround the flower tufts of Thyme, and they thus seem to teem with life. Activity is a warlike virtue, and is ever associated with true courage. On this notion, the ladies of the days of chivalry embroidered on the scarfs which they presented to their knights the figure of a bee hovering about a sprig of Thyme.

> I am not old,—though years have cast
>   Their shadows on my way;
> I am not old,—though youth has passed,
>   On rapid wings away.
> For in my heart a fountain flows,
> And round it pleasant thoughts repose;
> And sympathies, and feelings high,
> Spring like stars on evening's sky.
> Park Benjamin.

> The thrifty Thyme a home can find,
> Where smiles the sun, and breathes the wind.
> Mrs. Hale.

Take the instant way;
For honour travels in a strait so narrow,
Where one but goes abreast: keep then the path;
For emulation hath a thousand sons,
That one by one pursue: if you give way,
Or edge aside from the direct forthright,
Like to an entered tide, they all rush by,
And leave you hindmost.

Shakspeare.

The keen spirit
Seizes the prompt occasion,—makes the thought
Start into instant action, and at once
Plans and performs, resolves and executes.

Hannah More.

Come, I have learned, that fearful commenting
Is laden servitor to dull delay;
Delay leads impotent and snail-paced beggary.
Then fiery expedition be my wing,
Jove's Mercury, and herald for a king!
Go, muster men: my counsel is my shield:
We must be brief, when traitors brave the field.

Shakspeare.

Rouse thee! wake thy soul from sadness;
    Fail not in the eager strife!
See around the bright earth's gladness,—
    All activity and life!

Peerbold.

HOLLYHOCK.....*Ambition.*

WE have few flowers that contribute more to the ornamenting of large gardens than the Hollyhock, which, from its towering height and seeming love of display, is the emblem of ambition. The flowers are of all hues, from a blackish-purple to a faint white, and, though very beautiful, are without fragrance. They give gayety to the shrubbery until a late season of the year, throwing out a succession of flowers till the arrival of frost.

> Yet, press on!
> For it shall make you mighty among men;
> And, from the eyrie of your eagle thought,
> Ye shall look down on monarchs. Oh! press on!
> For the high ones and powerful shall come
> To do you reverence; and the beautiful
> Will know the purer language of your soul,
> And read it like a talisman of love.
> Press on! for it is godlike to unloose
> The spirit, and forget yourself in thought.
> > *Willis.*

> To the expanded and aspiring soul,
> To be but still the thing it long has been,
> Is misery, e'en though enthroned it were
> Under the cope of high imperial state.
> > *Joanna Baillie.*

Ay,—father!—I have had those earthly visions
And noble aspirations in my youth,
To make my own the mind of other men,
The enlightener of nations: and to rise
I knew not whither—it might be to fall;
But fall, even as the mountain cataract,
Which having leapt from its more dazzling height,
Even in the foaming strength of its abyss,
Lies low but mighty still.—But this is past,
My thoughts mistook themselves.

Byron.

I loved to hear the war-horn cry,
    And panted at the drum's deep roll;
And held my breath, when—flaming high—
I saw our starry banners fly,
As, challenging the haughty sky,
    They went like battle o'er my soul;
For I was so ambitious then,
I burned to be the slave—of men.

John Neal.

Know thou ambition is a restless flame,
Which ever strives to reach the high-placed stars!

Peerbold.

Ambition takes a thousand shapes among
Our race of Time's most valued toys, and yet
In court, in camp, in school, and mid the buzz
Of eager trade her spirit is the same.

C. Watson.

LAUREL.... *Glory.*

AMONG the ancient Greeks and Romans, the Laurel was consecrated to every species of glory. The beautiful shrub grows abundantly at Delphi, on the banks of the river Peneus. There its aromatic and evergreen branches shoot up to the height of the loftiest trees; and it is alleged that, by means of some secret virtue, they avert lightning from the spots which they adorn.

According to ancient fable, Daphne was the daughter of the river Peneus. Apollo fell in love with her, but she, preferring virtue to the love of the most eloquent of the gods, fled, in order to avoid the seducing magic of his words. Apollo pursued, and was on the point of overtaking her, when the nymph invoked her father, and was changed into a Laurel. The god, finding that he clasped an insensible tree in his arms, kissed its bright leaves. "Since thou canst not be my spouse," said he, "thou shalt, at least, be my tree." Thenceforward the Laurel was sacred to Apollo.

Ambition! ambition! I've laughed to scorn
   Thy robe and thy gleaming sword;
I would follow sooner a woman's eye,
   Or the spell of a gentle word.
But come with the glory of human mind,
   And the light of the scholar's brow,
And my heart shall be taught forgetfulness,
   And alone at thy altar bow.

Willis.

Give me the trumpet tone of fame,
The victor's wreath, the hero's name;
Though bites the steel and clanks the chain,
I would a warrior's glory gain,
A nation's pet and idol be,
With slaves to crouch and bend the knee.

W. H. C.

What is glory? What is fame?
The echo of a long-lost name;
A breath, an idle hour's brief talk;
The shadow of an arrant naught;
A flower that blossoms for a day,
    Dying next morrow;
A stream that hurries on its way,
    Singing of sorrow.

Motherwell.

In poet's lore, and sentimental story,
    It seems as 'twere this life's supremest aim
For heroes to achieve what men call glory,
    And die intoxicate with earth's acclaim.
Ah me! how little care the dead for breath
Of vain applause that saved them not from death.

MacKellar.

To die, and leave some worthy work to earth,
Is but a fine transition. 'Tis to leave
A talisman to call the spirit back,
Reft of its ground-born tenement.

C. Watson.

AMARANTH....*Immortality.*

THE Amaranth is unfading; and it has, therefore, been made the emblem of immortality. In Homer's time, it was customary to wear crowns of Amaranth at the funerals of distinguished personages. Milton, in his Lycidas, classes it among the flowers that "sad embroidery wear." In the floral games at Toulouse, the principal prize was a golden Amaranth for the best lyric composition. The Amaranthus hypochondriacus, one of the American species, is better known by the name of Prince's Feather.

There's a yearning that's felt in your heart's deepest cell,
And silently, vainly, within doth it swell;
And, scorning the hopes of the children of earth,
Seeks the bright home of its heavenly birth;
And that yearning, unquenched in the heart will lie,
Till refreshed by a draught from eternity.
Miss Larcom.

Oh, listen man!
A voice within us speaks that startling word,
"Man, thou shalt never die!" Celestial voices
Hymn it unto our souls: according harps,
By angel fingers touched, when the mild stars
Of morning sang together, sound forth still
The song of our great immortality.
Dana.

Immortal Amaranth! a flower which once
In paradise, fast by the tree of life
Began to bloom; but soon, for man's offence,
To heaven removed, where first it grew, there grows
And flowers aloft, shading the tree of life.

Milton.

There are distinctions that will live in heaven,
When time is a forgotten circumstance!
The elevated brow of kings will lose
The impress of regalia, and the slave
Will wear his immortality as free
Beside the crystal waters; but the depth
Of glory in the attributes of God
Will measure the capacities of mind;
And, as the angels differ, will the ken
Of gifted spirits glorify Him more.

Willis.

Were death annihilation—were this life
A lamp extinguished, ne'er to be relit,—
Then words of deep despondency were fit;
Then man perchance might lift his arm in strife
Against his LORD. Were blessedness of mind
Dependent on the vastness of the heap
Of gold and gems the schemers 'mong mankind
Could gather—then 'twere virtuous to weep.
But 'tis not so. Infinity of time
Is yet to be. Beyond our vision lie
Eternal realms, ineffably sublime
And beautiful.

MacKellar.

Strawberry....*Perfection*.

An eminent French author conceived the plan of writing a general history of nature, after the model of the ancients. A Strawberry plant, which, perchance, grew under his window, deterred him from this bold design. He examined the Strawberry, and, in so doing, discovered so many wonders, that he felt convinced the study of a single plant was sufficient to occupy a whole lifetime. He therefore gave up the pompous title which he had meditated for his work, and contented himself with calling it "Studies of Nature." The flowers of the Strawberry form pretty bouquets; but, as the delicious fruit is preferred to the flower, they are seldom plucked for that purpose. Among the glaciers of the Alps, the plants and flowers of the Strawberry are found in all seasons of the year. The plant seems to possess all the merits of plants, in their greatest perfection. The berries are the favourite accompaniment of the lordly feast and the most exquisite luxury of the rural repast. They vie in freshness and perfume with the buds of the sweetest flowers; delighting the eye, the taste, and smell, at the same time.

Let other bards of angels sing,
   Bright suns without a spot;
But thou art no such perfect thing:
   Rejoice that thou art not!

Wordsworth.

She's noble—noble, one to keep
Embalmed for dreams of fevered sleep.
An eye for nature—taste refined,
Perception swift—and balanced mind,—
And, more than all, a gift of thought
To such a spirit fineness wrought,
That on my ear her language fell
As if each word dissolved a spell.

Willis.

Oh! do not die, for we shall hate
    All women so when you are gone,
That thee I shall not celebrate,
    When I remember thou wast one.
But yet thou canst not die, I know;
    To leave this world behind is death;
But when thou from this world wilt go,
    The whole world vapours in thy breath.

Donne.

Were I to give my frolic fancy play,
I'd sing of her as some angelic sprite,
Who, wandering from her native home of light,
Fatigued, had fallen asleep upon the way;—
I'd fear to wake her, lest she'd plume her wings
And soar away from me and all sublunar things.

MacKellar.

SUNFLOWER....*False Riches.*

THE Sunflower has been thus named from the resemblance which its broad golden disk and rays bear
to the sun. The first Spaniards who arrived in Peru
were amazed at the profuse display of gold among the
people, but they were still more astonished when, in
May, they beheld whole fields covered with these
flowers, which they concluded, at first sight, must be
of the same precious metal. From this circumstance,
and the observation that gold, however abundant, cannot render a person truly rich, the Sunflower has been
made the emblem of false wealth. Many of the English
poets have adopted the notion that this flower ever turns
its face to the sun. Thomson, Moore, Darwin, and
Barton make a very fine use of the idea. But it is not
a fact. Those flowers which face the east at the opening of day, never turn to the west at the close of it.

> Searcher of gold, whose days and nights
>   All waste away in anxious care,
> Estranged from all of life's delights,
>   Unlearned in all that is most fair—
> Who sailest not with easy glide,
> But delvest in the depths of tide,
>   And strugglest in the foam;
> O! come and view this land of graves,
> Death's northern sea of frozen waves,
>   And mark thee out thy home.
>   *J. O. Rockwell.*

———

Think'st thou the man whose mansions hold
The worldling's pride, the miser's gold,
  Obtains a richer prize
Than he who in his cot, at rest,
Finds heavenly peace a willing guest,
And bears the earnest in his breast
  Of treasure in the skies?
Mrs. Sigourney.

Is all that heart requires, accomplished when
A heap of wealth is gathered at our door?
How thirsts the yearning soul for something more,
Some good that lies beyond its keenest ken!
MacKellar.

Can gold calm passion, or make reason shine?
Can we dig peace, or wisdom, from the mine?
Wisdom to gold prefer: for 'tis much less
To make our fortune, than our happiness.
Young.

It's no in titles nor in rank;
It's no in wealth like Lon'on bank,
  To purchase peace and rest;
It's no in making muckle mair:
It's no in books: it's no in lear,
  To make us truly blest:
If happiness hae not her seat
  And centre in the breast,
We may be wise, or rich, or great,
  But never can be blest.
Burns.

Heliotrope....*Devoted Affection.*

THE Heliotrope is a native of Peru. It is often confounded with the Sunflower, though it is of a different genus. The blossoms of the Heliotrope form clusters of very small, delicate, fragrant flowers, generally of a faint purple colour or white, sometimes red, or bluish-white. It is a general favourite of the fair sex, and is considered as the emblem of devoted affection, on account of its face being ever turned to the sun, which it seems to worship. The Heliotrope was introduced into Europe in 1740, by the celebrated Jussieu.

As laurel leaves, that cease not to be green,
From parching sonne, nor yet from winter's threat,—
As hardened oak, that fears no sworde so keen,—
As flint for tool, in twaine that will not fret,—
As fast as rock, or pillar surely set,—
So fast am I to you, and aye have been,
Assuredly whom I cannot forget;
For joy, for paine, for torment, nor for tene;
For loss, for gaine, for frowning, nor for threat;
For ever one, yea, both in calm and blast,
Your faithful love, and will be to the last!

Old Poet. 1555.

Yet do not think I doubt thee;
I know thy truth remains;
I would not live without thee,
For all the world contains.

Thou art the star that guides me
  Along life's troubled sea ;—
Whatever fate betides me,
  This heart still turns to thee.

G. P. Morris.

He on his side
Leaning half-raised, with looks of cordial love
Hung over her enamoured, and beheld
Beauty, which, whether waking or asleep,
Shot forth peculiar graces.

Milton.

Like Ixion,
I look on Juno, feel my heart turn to cinders
With an invisible fire ; and yet, should she
Deign to appear clothed in a various cloud,
The majesty of the substance is so sacred
I durst not clasp the shadow. I behold her
With adoration, feast my eye, while all
My other senses starve ; and, oft frequenting
The place which she makes happy with her presence,
I never yet had power, with tongue or pen,
To move her to compassion, or make known
What 'tis I languish for ; yet I must gaze still,
Though it increase my flame.

Massinger.

MIGNONETTE.....*Your Qualities surpass your Charms.*

THE Mignonette was introduced into Europe from Egypt, in 1750. It flowers from the beginning of spring until the end of autumn. Linnæus, who gave it the name of *Reseda odorata,* compares its perfume with that of ambrosia.

No gorgeous flowers the meek Reseda grace,
Yet sip, with eager trunk, yon busy race
Her simple cup, nor heed the dazzling gem
That beams in Fritillaria's diadem.

Evans.

I see her now within my view,—
A spirit, yet a woman too!—
Her household motions light and free,
And steps of virgin liberty;
A countenance in which do meet
Sweet records, promises as sweet;
A creature not too bright or good
For human nature's daily food.

Wordsworth.

Time has small power
. O'er features the mind moulds. Roses where
They once have bloomed a fragrance leave behind;
And harmony will linger on the wind;
And suns continue to light up the air,

MICNIONETTE PINK PINK-BUD

Your qualities surpassing your charms,
have drawn from me a confession of pure love

When set; and music from the broken shrine
Breathes, it is said, around whose altar-stone
His flower the votary has ceased to twine:—
Types of the beauty that, when youth is gone,
Breathes from the soul whose brightness mocks decline.
George Hill.

Rudely thou wrongest my deare heart's desire,
   In finding fault with her too portly pride;
The thing which I do most in her admire,
   Is of the world unworthy most envied.
For in those lofty looks is close implied
   Scorn of base things,—disdain of foul dishonour,
Threatening rash eyes which gaze on her so wide
   That loosely they ne dare to look upon her!
Spenser.

J<small>ASMINE</small>.....Amiability.

T<small>HE</small> Jasmine is a happy emblem of an amiable disposition. In all situations, it suffers the gardener to train its slender branches into any form he chooses: most commonly forming a living tapestry for arbours and garden walls, and everywhere throwing out a profusion of delicate and charming flowers, which perfume the air. The poets have showered their praise upon this plant, and all unite in considering it the emblem of the winsome quality of amiability. After paying a glowing tribute to the beauty and sweetness of the Violet, Thomas Miller, the "basket-maker" poet, thus speaks of the Jasmine:—

Stepping further into summer, comes the star-white Jasmine,—that sweet perfumer of the night, which only throws out its full fragrance when its sister stars are keeping watch in the sky; as if, when the song of the nightingale no longer cheered the darkness, it sent forth its silent aroma upon the listening air. Many a happy home does it garland, and peeps in at many a forbidden lattice, where Love and Beauty repose. Little did the proud courtiers and stately dames of Queen Elizabeth's day dream that this sweet-scented creeper (a sprig of which seemed to make the haughty haughtier still) would one day become 'so common as to cluster around and embower thousands of humble English cottages,—a degradation which, could they but have witnessed, would almost have made every plait of their starched ruffs bristle up, like "quills upon the fretful porcupine." Beautiful are its long, drooping, dark-green shoots, trailing around the trellis-work of a door-way, like a green curtain embroidered with silver flowers; while here and there the queenly Moss-Rose, creeping in and out like the threads of a fanciful tapestry, shows its crimson face amid the embowered green, —a beautiful lady peeping through a leaf-clad casement.

> A lover on the Indian Sea,
>   Sighing for her left far behind,
> Inhaled the scented Jasmine tree,
>   As it perfumed the evening wind:
> Shoreward he steered at dawn of day,
>   And saw the coast all round embowered,
> And brought a starry sprig away,
>   For her by whose green cot it flowered.

And oft when from that scorching shore,
 In after years those odours came,
He pictured his green cottage door,
 The shady porch, and window-frame,
Far, far away, across the foam :
 The very Jasmine-flower that crept
Round the thatched roof about his home,
 Where she he loved then safely slept.

Miller.

WOODBINE, OR HONEYSUCKLE....*Affection.*

THIS elegant, climbing shrub at once delights the
eye and gratifies the smell, by the exquisite fragrance
of its blossoms ; while it confers on those humble
dwellings in the rural districts of England and America,
a character of cheerfulness unknown in other countries. It begins to flower in May, and puts forth its
blossoms until the end of summer. It is chosen as the
emblem of affection, from its clinging to trees and lattices with all the ardour and constancy of a weak, confiding woman, clinging to one of the stronger, sterner
sex, in prosperity and in adversity.

Copious of flowers, the woodbine pale and wan,
But well compensating her sickly looks
With never-cloying odours, early and late.

Cowper.

Sister, sister, what dost thou twine?
I am weaving a wreath of the wild Woodbine;
I have streaked it without like the sunset hue,
And silvered it white with the morning dew:
And there is not a perfume which on the breeze blows
From the lips of the Pink or the mouth of the Rose,
That's sweeter than mine—that's sweeter than mine:
I have mingled them all in my wild Woodbine.
Miller.

   A Honeysuckle, on the sunny side,
   Hung round the lattices its fragrant trumpets.
Miss Landon.

   Ah! could you look into my heart,
     And watch your image there!
   You would own the sunny loveliness
     Affection makes it wear.
Mrs. Osgood.

The pensive soul with ardent thirsting turns
To heaven and earth to seek its fill of love.
MacKellar.

Oh! there is one affection which no stain
   Of earth can ever darken;—when two find,
The softer and the manlier, that a chain
   Of kindred taste has fastened mind to mind.
'Tis an attraction from all sense refined;
The good can only know it; 'tis not blind,
As love is unto baseness; its desire
Is but with hands entwined to lift our being higher.
Percival.

COWSLIP....*Pensiveness.*

THE solitary Cowslip was known to the old English poets as the "sweet nun of the fields," and has been immortalized in "Shakspeare's Midsummer Night's Dream." In America, the Cowslip may be found from Maine to Missouri. Its hues are not gaudy, but winning; and the whole appearance of the flower, as it blooms in some solitary vale, or on some gentle slope, expresses the idea of pensive beauty.

> The rose its blushes need not lend,
> Nor yet the lily with them blend,
>   To captivate my eyes:
> Give me a cheek the heart obeys,
> And, sweetly mutable, displays
>   Its feelings as they rise;
> Features, where pensive, more than gay,
> Save when a rising smile doth play,
>   The sober thoughts you see;
> Eyes that all soft and tender seem,
> And kind affections round them beam,
>   But most of all on me.
>
> *Frisbie.*

> There is a mood,
> (I sing not to the vacant and the young,)
> There is a kindly mood of melancholy
> That wings the soul, and points her to the skies.
>
> *Dyer*

8

Oh! fragrant dwellers of the lea,
   When first the wildwood rings
With each sound of vernal minstrelsy,
   When fresh the green grass springs!
What can the blessed spring restore
   More gladdening than your charms?
Bringing the memory once more
   Of lovely fields and farms!
Of thickets, breezes, birds, and flowers;
   Of life's unfolding prime;
Of thoughts as cloudless as the hours;
   Of souls without a crime.
Oh! blessed, blessed do ye seem,
   For, even now, I turned,
With soul athirst for wood and stream,
   From streets that glared and burned.
From the hot town, where mortal care
   His crowded fold doth pen;
Where stagnates the polluted air
   In many a sultry den.
And ye are here! and ye are here!
   Drinking the dew-like wine,
Midst living gales and waters clear,
   And heaven's unstinted shine.
I care not that your little life
   Will quickly have run through,
And the sward, with summer children rife,
   Keep not a trace of you.
For again, again, on dewy plain,
   I trust to see you rise,
When spring renews the wildwood strain,
   And bluer gleam the skies.

Again, again, when many springs
   Upon my grave shall shine,
Here shall you speak of vanished things,
   To living hearts of mine.

                 Mrs. Howitt.

Blest are the pure and simple hearts,
   Unconsciously refined,
By the free gifts that Heaven imparts
   Through nature to the mind ;
Not all the pleasures wealth can buy
Equal their happy destiny.

                 Mrs. Wells.

O Nature ! a' thy shows an' forms
To feeling, pensive hearts hae charms!
Whether the simmer kindly warms,
         Wi' life an' light,
Or winter howls, in gusty storms,
        The lang, dark night!

                 Burns.

     Melancholy
Sits on me, as a cloud along the sky,
Which will not let the sunbeams through, nor yet
Descend in rain, and end ; but spreads itself
'Twixt heaven and earth, like envy between man
And man—an everlasting mist.

                 Byron.

FORGET-ME-NOT.

THE name of this flower expresses clearly enough the meaning which is given to it. As a remembrancer it is universally received and eulogized. The name is derived from a German tradition, full of melancholy romance. It is related that a young couple, on the eve of being united, while walking along the banks of the Danube, saw a cluster of these flowers, floating on the stream, which was bearing it away. The affianced bride admired the beauty of the flower, and lamented its fatal destiny. The lover plunged into the water to secure it. No sooner had he caught it than he found himself sinking; but, making a last effort, he threw it on the bank at the feet of his betrothed, and, at the moment of disappearing for ever, exclaimed, "*Vergiss mein nicht!*" Since that event, this flower has been made emblematical of the sentiment, Forget-me-not. Its corollas are of a soft cerulean-blue colour, and it presents an interesting appearance as it grows along the banks of the rivers. The Forget-me-not is found in great perfection on the banks of a small stream near Luxembourg, in France. The stream is called the Fairies' Bath, and its banks are the favourite resort of festive parties.

That blue and bright-eyed floweret of the brook,
Hope's gentle gem—the fair Forget-me-not.
Coleridge.

Not on the mountain's shelving side,
  Nor in the cultivated ground,
Nor in the garden's painted pride,
  The flower I seek is found.
Where Time on sorrow's page of gloom
  Has fixed its envious lot,
Or swept the record from the tomb,
  It says Forget me not.
And this is still the loveliest flower,
  The fairest of the fair,
Of all that deck my lady's bower,
  Or bind her floating hair.

                  Göthe.

  Together they sate by a river's side,
    A knight and a lady gay,
And they watched the deep and eddying tide
    Round a flowery islet stray.
And, "Oh! for that flower of brilliant hue,"
    Said then the lady fair,
"To grace my neck with the blossoms blue
    And braid my nut-brown hair!"
The knight has plunged in the whirling wave
    All for his lady's smile:
And he swims the stream with courage brave,
    And he gains yon flowery isle.
And his fingers have cropped the blossoms blue,
    And the prize they backward bear;
To deck his love with the brilliant hue
    And braid her nut-brown hair.
But the way is long, and the current strong,
    And alas for that gallant knight!

For the waves prevail, and his stout arms fail,
  Though cheered by his lady's sight.
Then the blossoms blue to the bank he threw,
  Ere he sank in the eddying tide;
And "Lady, I'm gone, thine own knight true,
  Forget me not," he cried.
This farewell pledge the lady caught;
  And hence, as legends say,
The flower is a sign to awaken thought
  In friends who are far away.
For the lady fair of her knight so true,
  Still remembered the hapless lot:
And she cherished the flower of brilliant hue,
And she braided her hair with the blossoms blue
  And then called it "Forget-me-not!"

                  Mant.

To flourish in my favourite bower,
  To blossom round my cot,
I cultivate the little flower
  They call Forget-me-not.
This pretty little floweret's dye
  Of soft cerulean blue,
Appears as if from Ellen's eye
  It had received its hue.
Though oceans now betwixt us roar,
  Though distant be our lot,
Ellen! though we should meet no more,
  Sweet maid, Forget me not!

                  Anon.

Forget thee, love?—no, not while heaven
   Spans its starred vault across the sky;
Oh, may I never be forgiven,
   If e'er I cause that heart a sigh!
Sooner shall the Forget-me-not
   Shun the fringed brook by which it grows,
And pine for some sequestered spot,
   Where not a silver ripple flows.
By the blue heaven that bends above me,
Dearly and fondly do I love thee!
They fabled not in days of old
   That Love neglected soon will perish,—
Throughout all time the truth doth hold
   That what we love we ever cherish,
For when the Sun neglects the Flower,
   And the sweet pearly dews forsake it,
It hangs its head, and from that hour,
   Prays only unto Death to take it.
So may I droop, by all above me,
If once this heart doth cease to love thee!
The turtle-dove that's lost its mate,
   Hides in some gloomy greenwood shade,
And there alone mourns o'er its fate,
   With plumes for ever disarrayed:
Alone! alone! it there sits cooing:—
   Deem'st thou, my love, what it doth seek?
'Tis Death the mournful bird is wooing,
   In murmurs through its plaintive beak.
So will I mourn, by all above me,
If in this world I cease to love thee!

                    Miller.

Rosemary....*Remembrance.*

The Rosemary is so often mentioned by our early writers, both in prose, poetry, and our oldest dramas, that a long article, possessing great interest to such as love old-fashioned things, might be written upon it. The Rosemary was used both at their feasts and their funerals,—the christening-cup was stirred with it, and it was worn at their marriage ceremonies. Shakspeare has chosen it for the emblem of Remembrance, and who would attempt to change the meaning of a flower which his genius has hallowed, or disturb a leaf over which he has breathed his holy "superstition?"—in memory of him we use the latter word in all reverence. A few years ago it was customary, in many parts of England, to plant slips of Rosemary over the dead; nor has the practice yet fallen altogether into disuse—rural cemeteries will revive these ancient customs. Shakspeare chose the Rosemary as the emblem of affectionate remembrance, for its flowering in winter,—a very poetic and touching allusion. The sweet maniac, Ophelia, says,

There's Rosemary, "That for remembrance,
I pray you love, remember."

I loved thee, and must love thee still,
    In memory of the past
Amid whate'er of earthly ill
    My future lot is cast!

E'er in my boyhood's sunny prime,
When brightly from the urn of Time
  Life's golden moments fell,
Thou wert a peri to my eyes,
Sent from Love's own sweet paradise,
  In my young heart to dwell.

New York Mirror.

Remember me, I pray; but not
  In Flora's gay and blooming hour,
When every brake hath found its note,
  And sunshine smiles in every flower;
But when the falling leaf is sere,
  And withers sadly from the tree,
And o'er the ruins of the year
  Cold autumn weeps,—remember me.

Edward Everett.

The north wind howls; but, sheltered safe, and warm,
  Howl as it may, we feel secure from danger:
The fire burns blue, "betokening a storm"—
  A brand falls down, "precursor of a stranger."
My thoughtful mind runs o'er the track of years,
  When, tongs in hand, at our old hearth I sat,
And poked the embers, till my mother's fears
  Broke in upon the usual social chat,
"You'll fire the chimney, son!" The sparks would fly,
  Like little lumps of lightning up the flue,
And snap and crackle as they soared on high,
  As if they felt some pleasure in it too!
That fire is out—that hearth is cold—and they
Who felt its pleasant warmth have mostly passed away.

MacKellar.

ANEMONE....*Forsaken.*

ANEMONE was a nymph, beloved by Zephyr. Flora, jealous of her, banished her from her court, and transformed her into a flower, that blows before the return of spring. Zephyr has abandoned this unhappy beauty to the rude caresses of Boreas, who, unable to gain her love, harshly shakes her, half opens her blossoms, and causes her immediately to fade. An Anemone, with these words, *Brevis est usus*—"Her reign is short"—is touchingly expressive of the transitory nature of beauty.

In spring the green woods of merry England are covered with the flowers of the Anemone. Turn the eye whichever way you will, there it greets you like "a pleasant thought;" it forms a bed of flowers around the foot of the mighty oak, and below the tangling brambles, which you may peep between, but cannot pass,—there, also, are its pearly blossoms bending. The Greeks named it the flower of the Wind, and so plentiful is it in our country that we might fancy the breeze had blown it everywhere. The gaudy Anemone of the garden, the emblem of forsaken love, is known to all; but our favourites are the uncultivated offspring of the windy woods, which come long before the broad green leaves hang overhead to shelter them.

All flowers will droop in absence of the sun
That waked their sweets.

Dryden.

Farewell! I've loved thee much!—I feel
   That my idolatry was deep;
I know my heart can never heal,
   Till in the grave my passions sleep.
Yet I upbraid thee not, my love;
   'Twas all I had to offer thee,
   Love in its own simplicity.
How could I deem thou wouldst approve?
How hope to draw an angel from above?

                         Willis.

ACACIA....*Friendship.*

THE Acacia is a native of North America, from Canada to the Carolinas, and was consecrated by the Indians to the goddess of chaste love. Their bows were made of the incorruptible wood of this tree, and their arrows were pointed with its thorns. About a century ago, this tree was introduced into France by Robin, the botanist. It is a large, handsome tree, of quick growth, elegant foliage, and beautiful, rose-coloured blossoms.

   Celestial happiness! Whene'er she stoops
To visit earth, one shrine the goddess finds,
And one alone, to make her sweet amends
For absent heaven—the bosom of a friend,
Where heart meets heart, reciprocally soft,
Each other's pillow to repose divine.

                         Young.

The friend
Who smiles when smoothing down the lonely couch,
And does kind deeds, which any one can do
Who has a feeling spirit,—such a friend
Heals with a searching balsam.

Percival.

Lay this into your breast:
Old friends, like old swords, still are trusted best.

Webster.

O summer friendship,
Whose flattering leaves, that shadowed us in
Our prosperity, with the least gust drop off
In the autumn of adversity!

Massinger.

When thou art near,
The sweetest joys still sweeter seem,
The brightest hopes more bright appear,
And life is all one happy dream,
When thou art near.

Robert Sweney.

That friendship's raised on sand,
Which every sudden gust of discontent,
Or flowing of our passions, can change
As if it ne'er had been.

Massinger.

Moss....*Maternal Love.*

Moss is selected to be the emblem of maternal love, because, like that love, it glads the heart when the winter of adversity overtakes us, and when summer friends have deserted us. Rousseau, so long the prey of his own passions, and tormented by those of other men, soothed the latter years of his life by the study of nature. The Mosses, in particular, attracted his attention. It is these, he would say, that give a look of youth and freshness to the fields, at the moment when the flowers have gone to their graves. In winter the Mosses offer to the eye of the lover of nature their carpet of emerald green, their secret nuptials, and the charming mysteries of the urns and amphoræ which enclose their posterity. It is asserted that without the Mosses, part of our globe would be uninhabitable. At the northern extremity of the earth, the Laplanders cover their subterranean abodes with Moss, and thus defy the longest and most terrible winters. Their numerous herds of reindeer have no other food, yet they supply their owners with delicious milk, nutritious flesh, and warm clothing; thus combining for the poor Laplander all the advantages that we derive from the horse, cow, and sheep.

There is none
In all this cold and hollow world, no fount
Of deep, strong, deathless love, save that within
A mother's heart.

Mrs. Hemans.

The docile, swift Reindeer! Oh, when I was a child,
I loved all strange fantastic tales, the wondrous and the
      wild;
I read about the "Hundred Nights," in the Arabian
      Tales,
That tell of Genii, sprites, and dwarfs, of gold and dia-
      mond vales.
I read of Eastern gardens and palaces so rare,
And of Sultans and Sultanas, the cruel and the fair.
I read of Robin Crusoe! Ah! how I loved that book!
Nor even yet hath its strong charm wholly my mind
      forsook.
I read of voyages without end; of travels many too,
And fairy-tales and story-books—of these, good sooth,
      not few.
But I remember, more than all, I loved to think and
      hear
Of thee—thou strong and beautiful—thou swift and
      good Reindeer!
I remember in my earliest home, a dim antique beaufet,
And high upon its many shelves, things manifold were
      set.
Some piles of dark old books there were, amid the
      motley crowd,
And when tall enough to reach them, oh! glad was I,
      and proud.
And there I found old Æsop, whose fables we all know,
And Cookery-books of ancient dates, most grim and
      well worn too.
These I just peeped at, and put back—and still went
      groping on
Deep into that small mine of wealth that I so late had won.

Soon with some daring. tugs, I brought a lumbering
     volume slap
Down on the floor!   I sat down too, and dragged it on
     my lap.
The binding was antique and worn—the title-page was
     out,
And yet the treasure won from me a child's exultant
     shout;
For there were pictures many, of beast, and fish, and
     bird;
And *thou* wert there, thou good Reindeer, of whom so
     much I'd heard.
And that great heavy ancient book was such a prize
     to me!
It told me of the monstrous whale, and the small good
     honey-bee;
It told me of the elephant, the tiger, the gazelle,
Of the vast luxuriant jungles, and the lone, bright
     desert well;
Of humming-birds that sip the dew of flowers as they fly,
Of prairies wild, and wide, and green; of snowy moun-
     tains high:
I read there of the Northern sea, where iceberg islands
     float,
.And crush the great three-masted ship, as 'twere a
     cockle-boat;
I read about the harmless seals, and the shaggy Polar bear,
And the mighty troops of hungry wolves that roam and
     riot there.
I read of Nature's glorious works, and wondering went on,
And found before me pleasures, whose round will ne'er
     be done.

And in my good old-fashioned book I read of herb and
    tree,
That were food for man, and beast and bird, and for
    the honey-bee.
I read of grove-like banyans, of cedars broad and
    tall,
Of the lofty towering palm, and the Moss and lichen
    small.
And then I found how wondrously the poor Reindeer
    was fed,
When over all his frozen land deep winter's snow lay
    spread ;
How God had bid the barren ground produce this
    strange small thing,
On which whole countless herds of deer are ever pas-
    turing :
How, in the woods of scattered pine abundantly it
    grows,
And clothes the earth for many a mile beneath the
    trackless snows ;
How the sagacious Reindeer delves, and scents his on-
    ward way,
Till he reaches his scant mossy food, that doth his toil
    repay.
Oh! see him with his master's sledge! How swift ·
    they glide along,
Like a bird, or a fairy car I've read of, in some quaint
    old song.
Away! o'er the boundless snowy waste, so glittering
    and bright:
Away!—through the dark pine forest, as gloomy as
    the night:

Away o'er the frozen lake, the river, and the fen,
Away! Away!—Ye have winsome steeds, ye little
    Lapland men!
Ay, winsome steeds in sooth, with their antlers
    branched and high;
So sure of foot, and swift of pace, they truly seem to
    fly.
Ye need no palace-stables, no saucy pampered grooms,
To stretch your cracking purse-strings, and strut in
    liveried plumes;
No heavy half-year's bills, for oats, beans, straw, and
    hay.
The forest yields them lodgment, and food, where'er
    they stray.
And thus we find, in every clime, things beautiful and
    fair,
Each fitted to fulfil its task of use and beauty there;
And I remember thinking so, when, a little child, I
    read
The history of the good Reindeer, and the Moss whereon
    they fed.
                    Louisa A. Twamley.

Mother! dear mother! the feelings nurst
As I hung at thy bosom, clung round thee fast,
'Twas the earliest link in love's warm chain—
'Tis the only one that will long remain:
And as year by year, and day by day,
Some friend still trusted drops away,
Mother! dear mother! oh! dost thou see
How the shortened chain brings me nearer thee?
                    Willis.

Bishop Mant thus describes the place where Mosses grow:—

On upland hill, in lowland vale,
And where the frigid vapours sail,
Mantling the Alpine mountain hoar,
On granite-rock, or boggy moor,
On peat-clad marsh, or sandy heath,
On hillock's grassy slope ; beneath
The hedge-road fence, and on the bank,
Fringed with the plumed osier dank,
Of streamlet, pool, or waterfall ;
On wave-washed stone, on plastered wall ;
On tree of forest, or of fruit,
The bark-clad trunk, the heaving root ;
Or where the spring with oozing slime
Slides trickling down the rifted lime ;
Or where the grav'ly pathway leads
Through shady woods, o'er plashy meads :—
Exulting in the wintry cold,
Their cups the mossy tribes unfold ;
Fringed, and beneath a coping hid
Of filmy veil, and convex lid,
On many a thread-like stalk, bespread
With yellow, brown, or crimson red,
In contrast to the leaves of green,
A velvet carpet, where the queen
Of fairies might in triumph lie
And view the elvish revelry ;
Soft as the cygnet's downy plume,
Or produce of the silkworm's loom,
Survey them by the unaided eye,
And, if the seeds within you lie

Of love for natural beauty true,
They'll shoot enlivened at the view
Of hair or feather-mantled stem,
The waving stalk, the fringed gem,
Enveloping its chaliced fruit;
So fair, so perfect, so minute,
That bursting forth, the seeds may seem
A floating cloud of vapoury steam.
Or by the microscopic glass
Surveyed, you'll see how far surpass
The works of nature, in design,
And texture delicately fine,
And perfectness of every part,
Each effort of mimetic art.

A mother's love—how sweet the name!
  What is a mother's love?
—A noble, pure, and tender flame,
  Enkindled from above,
To bless a heart of earthly mould;
The warmest love that can grow cold;
  This is a mother's love.

Montgomery.

Dear mother, of the thousand strings which waken
  The sleeping harp within the human heart,
The longest kept in tune, though oft forsaken,
  Is that in which the mother's voice bears part;
Her still small voice bids e'en the careless ear
To turn with deep and pure delight to hear.

Miss E. J. Eames.

DANDELION....*The Rustic Oracle.*

THE Dandelion is the most common of flowers. It is
found in the four quarters of the globe, near the pole
as beneath the equator, on the margin of rivers and
streams as well as on sterile rocks. It serves the shepherd instead of a clock, while its feathery tufts are his
barometer, predicting calm or storm. The globes formed
by the seeds of the Dandelion are used for other purposes. If you are separated from the object of your
love, pluck one of those feathery spheres, charge each
of the little feathers with a tender thought; turn toward
the spot where the loved one dwells; blow, and the aërial
travellers will faithfully convey your secret message to
his or her feet. If you wish to know if that dear one
is thinking of you, blow again; and if a single aigrette
is left upon the stalk, it is a proof that you are not forgotten.

As thinks

The mariner of home,
When doomed through many a dreary waste
Of waters yet to roam,—
Thus doth my spirit turn to thee,
My guiding star o'er life's wild sea.

Mrs. Embury.

Dandelion, with globe of down,
The schoolboy's clock in every town,
Which the truant puffs amain,
To conjure lost hours back again.

Howitt.

PIMPERNEL....*The Weather-glass.*

THE COUNTRY MAID AND THE PIMPERNEL FLOWER.

"I'll go and peep at the Pimpernel,
And see if she think the clouds look well;
    For if the sun shine,
    And 'tis like to be fine,
    I shall go to the fair,
    For my sweetheart is there:
So, Pimpernel, what bode the clouds and the sky?
If fair weather, no maiden so merry as I."

Now the Pimpernel flower had folded up
Her little gold star in her coral cup,
    And unto the maid
    Thus her warning said:
    "Though the sun smile down,
    There's a gathering frown
O'er the checkered blue of the clouded sky;
So tarry at home, for a storm is nigh."

The maid first looked sad and then looked cross,
Gave her foot a fling, and her head a toss;
    "Say you so, indeed,
    You mean little weed?
    You're shut up for spite,
    For the blue sky is bright,
To more credulous people your warnings tell,
I'll away to the fair;—good day, Pimpernel.

———

"Stay at home! quoth the flower?—In sooth, not I;
I'll don my straw hat with a silken tie;
    O'er my neck so fair
    I'll a kerchief wear,
    White, chequered with pink,
    And then—let me think,
I'll consider my gown, for I'd fain look well:"
So saying, she stepped o'er the Pimpernel.

Now the wise little flower, wrapped safe from harm,
Sat fearlessly waiting the coming storm;
    Just peeping between
    Her snug cloak of green,
    Lay folded up tight,
    Her robe so bright;
Though 'broidered with purple, and starred with gold,
No eye might its bravery then behold.

The fair maiden straight donned her best array,
And forth to the festival hied away;
    But scarce had she gone
    Ere the storm came on;
    And, 'mid thunder and rain,
    She cried oft and again,
"Oh! would I had minded yon boding flower,
And were safe at home from the pelting shower."

Now, maidens, the tale that I tell would say,
Don't don fine clothes on a doubtful day,
Nor ask advice, when, like many more,
You had "made up your minds" some time before.
                    Louisa A. Twamley.

POPPY.... *Consolation.*

THE Red Poppy is the floral symbol of consolation.
The White Poppy is supposed to express, "My bane,
my antidote." The juice extracted from these plants
is employed to soothe the restless invalid to sleep, and
to ease the pangs of disease. According to the mythology of the Grecians, the Poppy owed its origin to
Ceres, who created it to assuage her grief, during her
search after her daughter Proserpine, who was carried
off by Pluto. The Poppy is extensively cultivated in
Europe, for the purpose of making opium from it.
Many species are cultivated in the garden. The double
flowers possess surpassing beauty, whether we consider
their delicate texture, elegance of shape, or variety of
colouring. In the time of Gesner, the celebrated botanist of Switzerland, the village Damons and Chloes
proved the sincerity of their lovers by placing in the
hollow of the palm of the left-hand, a petal, or flower-
leaf of the Poppy, which, on being struck by the other
hand, was broken with a sharp sound, which denoted
true attachment; but faithlessness, when it failed to
snap.

The world has closed its eyes and fallen asleep;
And GOD looks down from His eternal throne
And shuts the eye that long was wont to weep,
And makes the wretched feel they're not alone.
MacKellar

PRIDE AND THE POPPIES.—THEIR GRANDEUR AND FALL.

"We little Red-caps are among the corn,
Merrily dancing at early morn,
We know that the farmer hates to see
Our saucy red faces; but here are we!

"We pay no price for our summer coats,
Like those slavish creatures, barley and oats;
We don't choose to be ground and eat,
Like our heavy-head neighbour, Gaffer Wheat.

"Who dare thrash *us*, we should like to know!
Grind us, and bag us, and use us so!
Let meaner and shabbier things than we
So stupidly bend to utility!"

So said little Red-cap, and all the rout
Of the Poppy-clan set up a mighty shout;
Mighty for them, but if *you* had heard
You had thought it the cry of a tiny bird.

So the Poppy-folk flaunted it over the field,
In pride of grandeur they nodded and reeled;
And shook out their jackets, till naught was seen,
But a wide, wide shimmer of scarlet and green.

The Blue-bottle sat on her downy stalk,
Quietly smiling at all their talk.
The Marigold still spread her rays to the sun,
And the purple Vetch climbed up to peep at the fun.

The whimsical Bugloss, vain, beautiful thing,
Whose flowers, like the orient butterfly's wing,
Are deep, glowing azure, was eager to shed
O'er her yet unoped buds a delicate red;

First crimson, then purple, then loveliest blue;
E'en thrice doth she change her chameleon hue;
And she pities the flowers that grow merrily by,
Because in one dress they must bud, bloom, and die.

The homely Corn-cockle cared nothing, not she,
For the arrogance, bluster, and poor vanity
Of the proud Poppy-tribe, but she flourished and grew,
Content with herself, and her plain purple hue.

The sun went down, and rose bright on the morrow,
To some bringing joy, and to others e'en sorrow,
But blithe was the rich rosy farmer that morn
When he went with his reapers among the corn.

Forth went they betimes, a right merry band,
The sickles were glancing in each strong hand,
And the wealthy farmer came trotting along,
On his stiff little pony, mid whistle and song.

He trotted along, and he cracked his joke,
And chatted and laughed with the harvest-folk;
For the weather was settled, barometers high,
And heavy crops gladdened his practised eye.

"We'll cut this barley to-day," quoth he,
As he tied his white pony under a tree,

"Next to the upland wheat, and then the oats."
How the Poppies shook in their scarlet coats!

Ay, shook with laughter, not fear, for they
Never dreamed they too should be swept away,
And their laughter was spite, to think that all
Their "useful" neighbours were doomed to fall.

They swelled and bustled with such an air,
The corn-fields quite in commotion were,
And the farmer cried, glancing across the grain,
"How those rascally weeds have come up again!"

"Ha! ha!" laughed the Red-caps, "ha! ha! what a fuss
Must the poor *weeds* be in! how they're envying *us!*"
But their mirth was cut short by the sturdy strokes
They speedily met from the harvest-folks.

And when low on the earth each stem was laid,
And the round moon looked on the havoc made,
A Blue-bottle propped herself half erect,
And made a short-speech—to this effect.

"My dying kins-flowers, and fainting friends,
The same dire fate alike attends
Those who in scarlet or blue are dressed;
Then how silly the pride that so late possessed

"Our friends the Red-caps! how low they lie,
Who were lately so pert, and vain, and high!
They sneered at us and our plain array;
Are we now a whit more humbled than they?

"They scorned our neighbours :—the goodly corn
Was the butt of their merriment eve and morn,
They lived on its land, from its bounty fed,
But a word of thanks they never have said.

"And which is the worthiest now, I pray?
Have ye not learned enough to-day?
Is not the corn sheafed up with care,
And are not the Poppies left dying there?

"The corn will be carried and garnered up
To gladden man's heart both with loaf and cup;
And some of the seed the land now yields
Will be brought again to its native fields,

"And grow and ripen and wave next year
As richly as this hath ripened here;
And we poor weeds, though needed not,
Perchance may spring on this very spot.

"But let us be thankful and humble too;
Not proud and vain of a gaudy hue,
Ever remembering, though meanly drest,
That *usefulness* is of all gifts the best."
Louisa A. Twamley.

Will you drink of this fountain, and sorrow forget?
Has the past been so blest that you hesitate yet?
Can love, when 'tis slighted, still cherish a token,
Or hearts still forgive, that unkindness has broken?
Percival.

From a Poppy I have taken
Mortal's balm and mortal's bane;
Juice that, creeping through the heart,
Deadens every sense of smart;
Doomed to heal or doomed to kill,
Fraught with good or fraught with ill.

Mrs. Robinson.

ACANTHUS....*The Arts.*

THE Acanthus blooms in greatest perfection by the great rivers of hot climates. Among the ancients, it was a favourite, and they adorned their furniture, vases, and costly dresses, with its elegant leaves. When any obstacle obstructs the growth of the Acanthus, it puts forth fresh force and grows with additional vigour. Thus genius is strengthened by the difficulties which it cannot overcome. Callimachus, an ancient architect, derived the idea of the Corinthian capital, from seeing the leaves of an Acanthus surrounding a basket which had been set upon the ground, and impeded the regular growth of the plant.

Tired at first sight with what the muse imparts,
In fearless youth we tempt the heights of arts,
While from the bounded level of our mind
.Short views we take, nor see the length behind;
But, more advanced, behold with strange surprise
New distant scenes of endless science rise.

Pope.

For though I must confess an artist can
Contrive things better than another man,
Yet when the task is done, he finds his pains
Sought but to fill his belly with his brains.
Is this the guerdon due to liberal arts,
To admire the head and then to starve the parts?
Timely prevention though discreetly used
Before the fruits of knowledge were abused.
When learning has incurred a fearful damp,
To save our oil, 'tis good to quench the lamp.

Lady Alimony.

She had read
Her father's well-filled library with profit,
And could talk charmingly.   Then she would sing,
And play too, passably, and dance with spirit.
She sketched from nature well, and studied flowers,
Which was enough alone to love her for.
Yet she was knowing in all needlework,
And shone in dairy and in kitchen too,
As in the parlour.

James N. Barker.

Art became the shadow
Of the dear star-light of thy haunting eyes!
They called me vain, some mad—I heeded not,
But still toiled on, hoped on, for it was surest,
If not to win, to feel more worthy thee.

Bulwer. .

VALERIAN.....*An accommodating Disposition.*

THE Valerian was called by some of the old English writers the Setewale. It is generally found growing by ruined walls or buildings, and from the facility with which it propagates in these situations, it is made the emblem of an accommodating disposition. The root of the Valerian is considered a valuable remedy for many of those ailments which spring from luxurious living. It exerts a peculiar influence on the nervous system, revives the spirits, and strengthens the sight. The Valerian is too large and scrambling a plant to hold a place in the parterre of choice flowers.

How much more happy is that sweet estate,
   That neither creeps too low nor soars too high;
Which yields no matter for contempt or hate,
   Which others not disdain, nor yet envy,
Which neither does nor takes an injury,
   But living to itself in sweet content,
   Is neither abject, nor yet insolent.
                        1629.   *Herbert.*

My country, sir, is not a single spot
Of such a mould, or fixed to such a clime.
                               Miller.

MARVEL OF PERU....*Timidity.*

THE Marvel is a native of Peru, and receives its name
from the wonderful diversity of colours in flowers of
the same root;

> Changing from the splendid rose
> To the pale violet's dejected hue.
>
> *Akenside.*

This plant retains its beauty for a great length of time,
being frequently covered with blossoms from the beginning of July to the end of October. It is chosen
as the emblem of timidity, because the flowers are too
timid to expand during the day, and open and give out
their fragrance at night.

> Sure, 'twas his modesty. He might have thriven
> Much better possibly, had his ambition
> Been greater much. They ofttimes take more pains
> Who look for pins, than those who find out stars.
>
> *John Fountain.*

> I pity bashful men, who feel the pain
> Of fancied scorn and undeserved disdain,
> And bear the marks upon a blushing face
> Of needless shame and self-imposed disgrace.
>
> *Cowper.*

"Call back your odours, lonely flowers,
    From the night-wind call them back;
And fold your leaves till the laughing hours
    Come forth in the sunbeam's track.
The lark lies couched in her grassy nest,
    And the honey-bee is gone;
And all bright things are away to rest—
    Why watch ye here alone?"
Nay, let our shadowy beauty bloom,
    When the stars give quiet light;
And let us offer our faint perfume
    On the silent shrine of night.
Call it not wasted the scent we lend
    To the breeze when no step is nigh;
Oh! thus for ever the earth should send
    Her grateful breath on high!
And love us as emblems, night's dewy flowers,
    Of hopes unto sorrows given,
That spring through the gloom of the darkest hours,
    Looking alone to Heaven.

                    Mrs. Hemans.

That modest grace subdued my soul,
That chastity of look which seems to hang
A veil of purest light o'er all her beauties,
And by forbidding most inflames desire.

                    Young.

He saw her charming, but he saw not half
The charms her downcast modesty concealed.

                    Thomson.

ROSE BUD, YELLOW LILY, LILAC

Countless time majestic beauty
Has awakened my first emotions of love

STOCK....*Lasting Beauty.*

THE Stock has been made the emblem of lasting beauty; because, though it is less graceful than the rose, and less majestic than the lily, its splendour is more durable, and its fragrance of longer continuance. Few flowering plants have been so much and so rapidly improved by cultivation as the Stock. Within the last two centuries, its nature has been almost entirely changed by the florist; and it is now a shrub whose branches are covered with blossoms little inferior in dimensions to the rose. Stocks are produced of various colours, but the bright red or carmine must ever remain the favourite variety. The principal branches of this fragrant family are the Ten-week Stock, so named from flowering about ten weeks after it is sown; and the Brompton, which does not bloom till about twelve months after sowing, and was first cultivated in the neighbourhood of Brompton, England.

Without the smile from partial beauty won,
Oh, what were man!—a world without a sun!
Campbell.

Beauty has gone; but yet her mind is still
As beautiful as ever; still the play
Of light around her lips has every charm
Of childhood in its freshness.
Percival.

The lily may die on thy cheek,
  With freshness no longer adorning;
The rose that envelopes its whiteness may seek
  To take back her mantle of morning;
Yet still will Love's tenderness beam from thine eye,
And ask for that homage no heart can deny.
                           Dawes.

        The glory of the human form
Is but a perishing thing, and Love will droop
When its brief grace hath faded.   But the mind
Perisheth not, and when the outward charm
Hath had its brief existence, it awakes,
And is the lovelier that it slept so long.
                           Willis.

          Beauty lies
  As naturally upon his cheek as bloom
Upon a peach.   Like morning vapour, flies
  Before his smile my mind's infrequent gloom.
We tremble when we think that many a storm
  May beat upon him in the time to come,—
That his now beautiful and fragile form
  May bear a burden sore and wearisome.
Yet, so the stain of guiltiness and shame
Be never placed upon his soul and name,—
  So he preserve his virtue though he die,—
And to his God, his race, his country prove
  A faithful man, whom praise nor gold can buy,
Nor threats of vile, designing men can move,—
We ask no more.
                           MacKellar.

Scarlet Geranium.....*Stupidity.*

There are many varieties of the Geranium, distinguished by the shape and hue of the flowers and leaves, and the difference in their fragrance. The Scarlet Geranium is a very beautiful flower, but its scent is disagreeable. The following anecdote will give the reason of its being chosen as the emblem of stupidity. Madame de Staël was always angry when any of her acquaintance attempted to introduce a stupid person into her company. One day, one of her friends ventured to bring to her a young Swiss officer of most prepossessing exterior. The lady, pleased with his appearance, was very lively, and said a thousand flattering things to the new-comer, who seemed at first to be struck mute by surprise and admiration. When, however, he had listened to her for above an hour without opening his lips, she began to suspect the cause of his silence, and put to him such direct questions that he could not help answering. His answers were extremely silly! Madame de Staël, vexed at having thrown away her time and her wit, turned to her friend and said: "Indeed, sir, you are like my gardener, who thought to do me a pleasure by bringing me this morning a pot of Geranium: but I can tell you that I made him take back the flower, desiring him not to let me see it any more." "And why so?" asked the young man in astonishment. "It was, since you wish to know, because the Geranium is a beautiful scarlet flower; while

you look at it, it pleases the eye; but when you press
it ever so slightly, it gives out a disagreeable smell.
So saying, Madame de Staël rose and went out of the
room, leaving the young fool abashed and in confusion.

> This fellow is wise enough to play the fool;
> And to do that well, craves a kind of wit.
>
> *Shakspeare.*

> Your blunderer is as sturdy as a rock,
> The creature is so sure to kick and bite,
> A muleteer's the man to set him right.
> First appetite enlists him truth's sworn foe,
> Then obstinate self-will confirms him so.
> Tell him he wanders; that his error leads
> To fatal ill; that though the path he treads
> Be flowery, and he see no cause of fear,
> Death and the pains of hell attend him there.
> In vain the slave of arrogance and pride,
> He has no hearing on the prudent side.
> His still refuted quirks he still repeats;
> New raised objections with new quibbles meets;
> Till sinking in the quicksand he defends,
> He dies disputing, and the contest ends.
>
> *Cowper.*

> A set o' dull conceited hashes,
> Confuse their brains in college classes!
> They gang in stirks, and come out asses,
>   Plain truth to speak;
> An' syne they think to climb Parnassus
>   By dint o' Greek.

Gie me a spark o' Nature's fire,
That's a' the learning I desire ;
Then tho' I drudge thro' dub an' mire
           At pleugh or cart,
My muse, tho' hamely in attire,
           May touch the heart.
Burns.

The man who looks around him as he walks
  Sees objects often wonderful and new ;
And he who thinks while his companion talks
  In time may grow the wiser of the two.
An open eye—a quick, attentive ear
  Will lead the mind into the ways of knowledge ;
  For all the world's a universal college,
And every one may be a learner here.
Experience is the teacher : dear, indeed,
Her charges are to thoughtless folks and fools ;
But those who follow carefully her rules
  The various tongues of nature learn to read.
Who seldom ploughs his mind shall reap but little ;
  Weeds quickly overspread the fallow soil ;
  The toiler may be wearied by his toil,
But it shall yield sufficiency of victual,
  Enough for his own use, and much to spare.
To him who hath, abundance shall be given ;
  From him who squanders wastefully his share,
All that he has shall righteously be riven :
  The world shall make a proverb of his name,
  And he shall fill a sepulchre of shame.
MacKellar.

Oak Geranium....*Friendship.*

THE Oak Geranium does not present so beautiful an appearance as the scarlet variety; but the pale blue colour of the flower, and the length of time which it continues in bloom, endear it to us as the emblem of true friendship.

What though on Love's altar the flame that is glowing
  Is brighter?—yet Friendship's is steadier far!
One wavers and turns with each breeze that is blowing,
  And is but a meteor,—the other's a star!
      In youth Love's light
      Burns warm and bright,
  But dies ere the winter of age be past,—
      While Friendship's flame
      Burns ever the same,
  And glows but the brighter, the nearer its last!

Anon.

    Thanks to my stars, I have not ranged about
    The wilds of life, ere I could find a friend:
    Nature first pointed out my brother to me,
    And early taught me, by her sacred force,
    To love thy person, ere I knew thy merit,
    Till what was instinct grew up into friendship.
    Ours has severest virtue for its basis,
    And such a friendship ends not but with life.

Addison.

O! Friendship! in thy constant ray,
  My heart is cheered and cannot sink,
Though gloom and storm around me play
  And I am pressed to death's cold brink!
                              Peerbold.

                    The friend
Who smiles when smoothing down the lonely couch,
And does kind deeds, which any one can do
Who has a feeling spirit,—such a friend
Heals with a searching balsam.
                              Percival.

Delightful is an evening's cheerful chat
  With pleasant friends, especially to one
  Who has been long away.   The minutes run
With speed that all the talkers marvel at.
So much to talk about—so much to tell—
So many sleeping memories to awaken—
  The various fates that absent friends befell—
Whom time has spared, and whom the grave has taken;
  The tear to shed for those who've passed away—
  The sigh to breathe for those who've gone astray—
Our times of darkness, and our days of light—
  Our purposes and plans for coming years—
  Our heavenly hopes, our earthly human fears—
And lo! 'tis time to say, "Good-night, dear friends,
  good-night!"
                              MacKellar.

Tuberose.....*Dangerous Love.*

THE superb Tuberose is a native of the East Indies and South America, and was introduced into Europe in 1632. It has since spread all over the world. The flower is of a white colour, sometimes tinged with a blush of pink. Its perfume is delicious and powerful; but if you would enjoy it without danger, keep at some distance from the plant. If you come with the object of your affection to inhale its perfume by moonlight, when the nightingale is pouring forth its ravishing melody, these odours will add an inexpressible charm to your enjoyment; but, if, regardless of the precepts of moderation, you approach too near, this divine flower will then be but an enchantress who will pour a dangerous poison into your bosom. Thus the love which comes from above purifies and exalts; but that which springs from earth debases and proves the bane of imprudent youth.

Yes, Love is but a dangerous guest
   For hearts as young as thine,
Where youth's unshadowed joys should rest,
   Life's spring-time fancies shine.
Then, sweetest, leave the wildering dream,
   Till Time has nerved thy heart ·
To brook the fitful cloud and gleam,
   Which must in love have part.

               Mrs. Osgood.

The Tuberose, with her silvery light,
  That in the gardens of Malay
Is called the mistress of the night,
So like a bride, scented and bright,
  She comes out when the sun's away.

Moore.

If all the world and love were young,
And truth in every shepherd's tongue,
These pleasures might my passions move,
To live with thee and be thy love.
So fading flowers in every field,
To winter floods their treasures yield;
A honeyed tongue, a heart of gall,
Is fancy's spring, but sorrow's fall.

Sir Walter Raleigh.

      Instability and change are written
On us and all our works. The loveliest things,
  When full of promise, oftentimes are smitten;
And sweetest roses foster hidden stings.
  The world, if loved too well, doth ever pall,
And the poor fool who set his heart thereon
  Is doomed to see his hope in ruins fall,
Its frail foundation undermined and gone.

MacKellar.

Dahlia.....*Elegance and Dignity.*

THE Dahlia is a native of South America, but is now
extensively cultivated in Europe and North America.
The shrub grows to a considerable height, and the
flowers are large and beautiful. The most common
colours are crimson and purple. No more appropriate
emblem of elegance and dignity of carriage could have
been selected. These qualities strike us at the first
view of the Dahlia.

I loved thee for thy high-born grace,
  Thy deep and lustrous eye—
For the sweet meaning of thy brow,
  And for thy bearing high.
I loved thee for thy stainless truth,
  Thy thirst for higher things,
For all that to our common lot
  A better temper brings.
And are they not all thine—still thine?
  Is not thy heart as true?
Holds not thy step its noble grace?
  Thy cheek its dainty hue?
And have I not an ear to hear?
  And a cloudless eye to see—
And a thirst for beautiful human thought,
  That first was stirred by thee?

                              Willis.

Why, a stranger—when he sees her,
In the street even smileth stilly,
Just as you would at a lily.

Miss Barrett.

Her grace of motion and of look, the smooth
And swimming majesty of step and tread,
The symmetry of form and feature, set
The soul afloat, even like delicious airs
Of flute and harp.

Milman.

Her glossy hair was clustered o'er a brow
Bright with intelligence, and fair and smooth;
Her eyebrow's shape was like the aërial bow,
Her cheek all purple with the beam of youth,
Mounting, at times, to a transparent glow,
As if her veins ran lightning.

Byron.

Do but look on her eyes! they do light
  All that love's world compriseth;
Do but look on her hair! it is bright
  As love's star, when it riseth!
Do but mark,—her forehead's smoother
Than words that soothe her!
And from her arched brows such a grace
Sheds itself through the face,
As alone there triumphs to the life,
All the gain, all the good, of the element's strife.

Jonson.

CAMELLIA JAPONICA....*Modest Merit.*

· THE Camellia Japonica is a native of China and
Japan. It is a large, evergreen tree. The flowers are
large, of the form of a rose of variegated hues—the red
prevailing—and, without fragrance. It is made the
emblem of modest worth, because, as Roscoe observes,
"it boasts no fragrance, and conceals no thorn."

> Let other bards of angels sing,
>   Bright suns without a spot;
> But thou art no such perfect thing,
>   Rejoice that thou art not.
> True beauty dwells in deep retreats,
>   Whose veil is unremoved;
> Till heart with heart in concord beats,
>   And the lover is beloved.
>   *Wordsworth.*

Oh, that estates, degrees, and offices,
Were not derived corruptly! and that dear honour
Were purchased by the merit of the wearer!
How many then should cover, that stand bare?
How many be commanded, that command?
How much low peasantry would then be gleaned
From the true seed of honour? and how much honour
Picked from the chaff and ruin of the times,
To be new varnished?
                                  Shakspeare.

There's a proud modesty in merit!
Averse from asking, and resolved to pay
Ten times the gift it asks.

Dryden.

Oh, your desert speaks loud; and I should wrong it,
To lock it in the wards of covert bosom;
When it deserves with characters of brass
A forted residence 'gainst the tooth of time,
And razure of oblivion.

Shakspeare.

Thine is a mind of maiden artlessness!
    Unstained, undarkened, by the dross of earth;
A soul, that through thine eyes, bright beams express
    Thy nature, e'en as noble as thy birth;
Whose every glance reflects the gem enshrined,
Worthy a form so fair; the diamond of the mind.

Anon.

His resting-place is noted by a stone
Of whitest marble: truthful words are those
Inscribed thereon. The scene of his repose
Befits his life: 'twas beautiful and calm.
In meekness and in love he went his way,
Uprightly walking—filling up the day
With useful deeds. He often poured the balm
Of healing into wounded breasts; nor sought
The praise of men in doing good.

MacKellar.

THORN-APPLE....*Deceitful Charms.*

THE flowers of the Thorn-Apple droop while the sun shines beneath their dull-looking foliage, but on the approach of night, they revive, display their charms, and unfold their prodigious bells, which nature has coloured with purple, lined with ivory; and to which she has given an odour that attracts and intoxicates, but is so dangerous as to stupify those who inhale it even in the open air. It is a dangerous plant to be allowed to grow where children go, as the beauty of its flowers and fruit is liable to tempt them to their destruction; since it possesses so poisonous a quality as to produce paralysis, and even madness, in those who have eaten it. Its leaves have been recommended for coughs and asthma. The charms of the Thorn-Apple flower are beautiful, but deadly; like those of the corrupt and treacherous, to be found in every society.

But pleasures are like poppies spread,
You seize the flower, its bloom is shed;
Or like the snow-falls in the river,
A moment white—then melts for ever;
Or like the borealis race,
That flit ere you can point their place;
Or like the rainbow's lovely form
Envanishing amid the storm.

Burns.

O serpent heart, hid with a flowering face!
Did ever dragon keep so fair a cave?

Shakspeare.

     Get thee glass eyes;
And like a scurvy politician, seem
To see the things thou dost not.

Shakspeare.

Women of kind have conditions three:
 The first is,—they be full of deceit,
To spinne also is their property,
 And women have a wonderful conceit,
For they can weep oft, and all is a sleight,
And ever when they list, a tear is in the eye,
Beware, therefore,—the blind eateth many a fly.

Chaucer.

Ah, that deceit should steal such gentle shapes,
And with a virtuous visor hide deep vice!

Shakspeare.

Smooth runs the water, where the brook is deep;
And in his simple show he harbours treason.
The fox barks not, when he would steal the lamb.
No, no, my sovereign; Gloster is a man
Unsounded yet, and full of deep deceit.

Shakspeare.

LADY'S SLIPPER....*Capricious Beauty.*

THE Lady's Slipper is well known in Europe and
America. The plant is small, but produces a considerable number of flowers, of variegated hues. This
flower is made the emblem of capricious beauty, because
she seems,

——With her changeful hues,
As she were doubtful which array to choose.

I saw thee in the gay saloon
   Of Fashion's glittering mart,
Where Mammon buys what Love deplores,
   Where Nature yields to Art;
And thou wert so unlike the herd
   My kindling heart despised,
I could not choose but yield that heart,
   Though Love were sacrificed.
The smile which hung upon thy lips,
   In transport with their tone,
The music of thy thoughts, which breathed
   A magic theirs alone!
The looks which spake a soul so pure,
   So innocent and gay,
Have passed, like other golden hopes
   Of happiness, away.

Dawes.

Her eyes
Are blue and beautiful, and flash out gleams
Of diamond light, like that which brightly beams
On stilly summer nights from starlit skies.
Her cheeks are tinted with the blushing dyes
Which Heaven—so wisely bountiful—bestows
In virgin freshness on the modest rose. ·

MacKellar.

Most fair is e'er most fickle.   A fair girl
Is like a thousand beauteous things of earth,
But most like them in love of change.

Peerbold.

We gaze and turn away, and know not where,
Dazzled and drunk with beauty, till the heart
Reels with its fulness.

Byron.

Beauty gives
The features perfectness, and to the form
Its delicate proportions: she may stain
The eye with a celestial blue—the cheek
With carmine of the sunset; she may breathe
Grace into every motion, like the play
Of the least visible tissue of a cloud:
She may give all that is within her own
Bright cestus—and one glance of intellect,
Like stronger magic, will outshine it all.

Willis.

11

Althea....Consumed by Love.

The name and signification of the Althea is derived
from the Grecian fable of Althea and her son, who lost
his life in consequence of his love for the beautiful
Atalanta. His consuming away as the fatal brand was
burning, suggested the emblem of consumed by love.
The Althea is a shrub from five to seven feet in height,
and is a native of the East Indies. The flowers are
about the size of the common rose, and either of a white
or pink hue.

There is an all-consuming passion here;
But 'tis a vestal flame, which worships thee!

Anon.

Like Ixion,
I look on Juno, feel my heart turn to cinders
With an invisible fire; and yet should she
Deign to appear clothed in a various cloud,
The majesty of the substance is so sacred
I durst not clasp the shadow. I behold her
With adoration, feast my eye, while all
My other senses starve; and oft, frequenting
The place which she makes happy with her presence,
I never yet had power, with tongue or pen,
To move her to compassion, or make known
What 'tis I languish for; yet I must gaze still,
Though it increase my flame.

Massinger.

With thee conversing, I forget all time;
All seasons and their change, all please alike.

Milton.

Love is a region full of fires,
And burning with extreme desires;
An object seeks, of which possest,
The wheels are still, the motions rest,
The flames in ashes lie opprest;
The meteor, striving high to rise,
The fuel spent, falls down and dies.

Beaumont.

What scenes appear where'er I turn my view!
The dear ideas, where'er I fly, pursue,
Rise in the grave, before the altar rise,
Stain all my soul, and wanton in my eyes.
I waste the matin lamp in sighs for thee,
Thy image steals between my God and me;
Thy voice I seem in every hymn to hear,
With every bead I drop too soft a tear.
When from the censer clouds of fragrance roll,
And swelling organs lift the rising soul,
One thought of thee puts all the pomp to flight,
Priests, tapers, temples, swim before my sight:
In seas of flame my plunging soul is drowned,
While altars blaze, and angels tremble round.

Pope.

Larkspur....*Flights of Fancy.*

Larkspur, Lark's-claw, Lark-heels, and Lark's-toe
have been given in allusion to the long spur-like nectary, which has been whimsically supposed to represent
these things, and many more. The Latin name, *Del-*
phinium, is from the Greek, Dolphin, because the nectary was thought like that fish. The French call it
Dauphinelle, pied d'alouette, l'éperon de chevalier, (knight's
spur;) and the Italian, *speronella,* (little spur,) *sperone*
di cavaliere, (knight's spur,) and *fior regio,* (king-flower.)
These names give quite a chivalric importance to the
gentle flower, and furnish abundant subject for thought
and fancy. Our own rural names give us a picture of
the sky-lark; that "musical cherub," soaring far and
high into the blue summer heaven, above the lonely
mountain-top, or over the busy town, and we can recall
the delight of listening to his sweet melody.

Louisa A. Twamley.

For never yet was bosom found
So dull of sense to music's sound,
As not to linger on the way,
And list to his ascending lay,
And upward gaze with straining sight,
And see him melting into light;
Till the eye fail its part to bear
In concert with the hearing ear;

And naught remain but what may seem
Imagination's fairy dream,
Or the sweet strain, if such there were,
Of Prospero's spirit in the air.
Oh, for that strength of voice and wing
To sing and soar, to soar and sing;
With all his joyousness of heart
From earth's encumbrances apart;
And with heaven's denizens on high
To revel mid the calm clear sky!

Mant.

Fancy is a fairy, that can hear,
Ever, the melody of nature's voice,
And see all lovely visions that she will.

Mrs. Osgood.

All impediments in fancy's course
Are motives of more fancy.

Shakspeare.

Ever let the fancy roam,
Pleasure never is at home;
Then let winged Fancy wander
Through the thoughts still spread beyond her:
Oh, sweet Fancy! let her loose,
Every thing is spoilt by use.

Kent.

Dyer's Weed....*Relief.*

Dyer's Weed is like a very large upright plant of Mignonette, to which sweet exotic it is nearly related, both being members of the *reseda* family. The *Reseda odorata*, or Mignonette, is a native of Egypt, and was introduced into England in 1752. The word *reseda* is from *resedo*, to calm, to appease. The plants were thought useful applications to external bruises, to ease pain. There are two species growing wild in England. *Reseda lutea*, or Base-rocket, likes a chalky soil, but *R. luteola*, the Dyer's Weed, is often found on waste ground everywhere. It is much used by dyers, particularly in France. It affords a most beautiful yellow dye, for cotton, woollen, mohair, silk, and linen. Blue cloths dipped in a decoction of it become green. The entire plant, when about to flower, is pulled up, and employed both fresh and dried. Like the Coltsfoot, this plant is among the first which spring from the rubbish thrown out of coal-pits. Linnæus observed, that the nodding spike of flowers always follows the sun, even on a cloudy day, pointing eastward in a morning, southward at noon, westward in the afternoon, and northward at night. If this be true, it may supplant the sunflower in the favour of sentimental florists, for the inconstancy of that has long been proved. Good old Gerarde, who evidently did his best to believe all things, says, that he has seen four sunflowers on one stem, pointing to the four cardinal points. I am wandering from my subject, but must remind you of some sweet lines by that poet of nature—Clare, where he groups the sunflower so nicely; and you may look at that cottage, where the children are playing, and see the picture nearly realized:

Where rustic taste at leisure trimly weaves
The rose and straggling woodbine to the eaves,
And on the crowded spot that pales enclose
The white and scarlet daisy rears in rows,
Training the trailing peas in clusters neat,
Perfuming evening with a luscious sweet,
And sun-flowers planting for their gilded show,
That scale the window's lattice ere they blow,
And, sweet to habitants within the sheds,
Peep through the crystal panes their golden heads.

A gentle peace, like evening winds
  In summer from the ocean's breast,
Moved o'er my sighing, sinking soul,
  And soothed my murmuring griefs to rest;
And through the weary night of pain,
  When it were manliness to weep,
My soul was comforted by this—
  "He giveth his beloved sleep."

MacKellar.

NASTURTION....*Patriotism.*

THE Nasturtion is a native of Europe and the East. The flowers are of a very brilliant golden yellow, and present a beautiful appearance. The plant is said to emit flashes of light in the morning before sunrise, and also at twilight. Its pure, glowing hue recalls that ardent feeling, so clear of self, which leads men to lay down their lives and fortunes for their country's safety and glory.

Land of the forest and the rock,
  Of dark blue lake and mighty river—
Of mountain reared aloft to mock
The storm's career and lightning's shock,
  My own green land forever!
                              Whittier.

Clime of the daring, thy sheltering banner
  Unfurls its stars o'er the land and the sea;
While tyrants are warring, and freemen love honour,
  That banner shall be the light of the free.
                              C. Watson.

Our country first, their glory and their pride,
Land of their hopes, land where their fathers died,
When in the right, they'll keep thy honour bright,
When in the wrong, they'll die to set it right.
                              James T. Fields.

Pride in the gift of country and of name
  Speaks in the eye and step—
  He treads his native land!

Halleck.

The patriot! go, to Fame's proud mount repair,
The tardy pile, slow rising there,
With tongueless eloquence shall tell
Of them who for their country fell.

Sprague.

'Tis home-felt pleasure prompts the patriot's sigh,
This makes him wish to live, and dare to die.

Campbell.

Land where he learned to lisp a mother's name,
The first beloved in life, the last forgot,
  Land of his frolic youth,
  Land of his bridal eve,
Land of his children—vain your column's strength,
Invaders! vain your battles' steel and fire!
  Choose ye the morrow's doom—
  A prison or a grave!

Halleck.

My country is my Holy Land.   I love her!
The purest, brightest skies are spread above her,
And heavenliest verdure covers vale and hill.
The clearest waters fish did ever swim in
Are hers. And oh, what words can praise her virtuous
    women?

MacKellar.

NIGHTSHADE, OR BITTER-SWEET....*Truth.*

ACCORDING to the belief of the ancients, Truth was the mother of Virtue, the daughter of Time, and queen of the world. It is a frequent saying, that Truth lies at the bottom of a well, and that she always mingles some bitterness with her sweet blessings; and we have chosen for her emblem a plant which, like her, delights in the shade, and is evergreen. The Nightshade is the only plant in England which loses and reproduces its leaves twice a year.

> Truth, crushed to earth will rise again,
>   The eternal years of God are hers;
> But Error, wounded, writhes with pain,
>   And dies among her worshippers.
>
> *Bryant.*

> The pure deep sky above may figure Truth;
> Though mists and clouds may long obscure its face,
> Gaze with patience, and ere long they'll pass.
>
> *Peerbold.*

> 'Tis not enough your counsel shall be true;
> Blunt truths more mischief than nice falsehoods do.
> Men must be taught as if you taught them not,
> And things unknown proposed as things forgot.
> Without good breeding, truth is disapproved;
> That only makes superior sense beloved.
>
> *Pope.*

Truth needs no flowers of speech.

Pope.

When fiction rises pleasing to the eye,
Men will believe, because they love the lie;
But truth herself, if clouded with a frown,
Must have some solemn proofs to pass her down.

Churchill.

All truth is precious, if not all divine,
And what dilates the powers must needs refine.

Cowper.

Verily there is nothing so false, that a sparkle of truth
is not in it.

Tupper.

This above all, to thine own self be true;
And it must follow, as the night the day,
Thou canst not then be false to any man.

Shakspeare.

What is truth?—a staff rejected.

Wordsworth.

It is a weary and a bitter task
Back from the lip the burning word to keep,
And to shut out heaven's air with falsehood's mask,
And in the dark urn of the soul to heap
Indignant feelings—making e'en of thought
A buried treasure.

Mrs. Hemans.

The Sweet Flag—Acorus Calamus....*Grace.*

One autumn eve I sat alone
　　Beside my study fire;
I'd written long, and eyes and head
　　And fingers 'gan to tire.

I rose to shut my desk, and go—
　　Quite weary—half asleep—
A book fell open as I moved;
　　E'en sleepy eyes must peep;

And, pictured on its page, I saw
　　The portrait of a friend,
Whose smiling face bade my dull thoughts
　　To happy memories wend.

It was the tall, sweet-scented Flag,
　　Lay pictured there so true,
I could have deemed some fairy hand
　　The faithful image drew.

The falchion-leaves, all long and sharp;
　　The stem, like a tall leaf too,
Except where, halfway up its side,
　　A cone-shaped flower-spike grew,

Like a lady's finger, taper, long,
　　From end to end arrayed

In close scale-armour, that was all
  Of starry flowers made.

If you could fancy fairy folk
  Would mimic works of ours,
You'd think their dainty fingers here
  Had wrought mosaic flowers.

The tiny petals, neatly formed,
  With geometric skill,
Are each one so exactly shaped,
  Its proper place to fill.

And stamens, like fine golden dust,
  Spangle the flowerets green;
Aught more compact and beautiful,
  Mine eyes have never seen!

How well I know when first I met
  The Sweet Flag's graceful form;
'Twas on a glowing summer's day,
  Mid hearts as bright and warm.

Mid hearts as warm as sunny gleams,
  And eyes as kind and bright,
And spirits that, like sunshine too,
  Are cheering, loved, and light.

We gathered there the Acorus
  From Claremont's quiet lake;
And home with me, full many a mile,
  I did the pale flower take.

'Twas new to me, but yet is not
  So very scarce and rare,
As many a river knoweth well;
  None better than the Yare!

For by its banks abundantly
  The fragrant tall leaves grow;
Singing with reedy rustling voice,
  Whene'er soft breezes blow.

The Mayor of Norwich holds in June
  His annual feast and show;
And to the grand cathedral church
  Processions with him go.

And then the gray and solemn aisles,
  And all the ancient floor,
Are with the aromatic leaves
  Bestrewèd thickly o'er.

In by-gone days the costly fumes
  Of incense here were shed;
But sweeter far the fragrant gush
  That greets each passing tread.

In the sordid streets are bowers built,
  Of these same reeds as well,
Plaited and wrought like basket-work,
  All full of spicy smell.

And many a queer and quaint device
  Are round about them made,

Of the gold and red ranunculus,
   In varied shape and shade.

Oh! many a young and guileless heart
   Is blithe as blithe can be,
To walk through Norwich streets that morn,
   The decked out bowers to see.

In far gone times, ere folks had grown
   So mighty nice and clever—
When carpets were unheard-of things,
   And druggets dreamed of never—

When wide bare floors of good hard mud
   Or stone, not over even,
Were all that unto knightly strides,
   Or dames' light steps, were given—

When common rushes strewed the halls
   Where royal banquets were—
How precious must these reeds have been
   Beside the banks of Yare!

I can fancy high and dainty dames
   Sending stout serving-men
To gather store of these sweet Flags,
   From river, pool, and fen.

Perhaps to strew a lady's bower,
   Perhaps the castle hall,
Where warlike lords and knights should meet
   At stately festival.

How often in the chapel too,
  The fresh-thrown reeds might lie;
While the tears and smiles of a bridal band
  Went softly passing by!

And they were there when sorrow deep
  Wept the untimely doom
Of young, and bright, and beautiful,
  Borne to the ancestral tomb.

In sooth it is an ancient thing,
  This new-found friend of mine,
And many a scene of joy and wo
  Hath it known in days lang syne.

I love it for them all right well,
  But yet I love it more
For the fairy scene that lay around
  Its home on that lakeless shore:

Beside the bank the stately trees
  Waved gently to and fro,
And flitting specks of sunlight fell
  The leafy branches thro',

And danced among the tall keen reeds,
  And on the water fell,
Where the merry fish were glancing swift;
  And the water snake, as well,

Came, gliding in a graceful curl
  All silently and still,

Like a lord in his own dominions there,
    Swimming about at will.

Now toward the margin where we stood
    We saw him steering on,—
Then under groups of lily leaves
    The happy thing was gone.

And wild-fowl, water-rats, and all,
    Lived in that little lake;
Oh, what a pleasant picture now
    My thoughts of it awake!

Its margent of smooth lawny turf
    Was mossy, soft, and deep,
Where the shadows broad of the beech and oak
    Seemed quietly to sleep.

The rhododendrons, purple yet
    With many a massive wreath,
Had seedling plants, a countless host,
    Crowding the turf beneath.

I dearly love small relics brought
    From spots where I have been,
That seem to certify the facts
    Of memory's pictured scene;

But seeds and roots of flowers are
    The pleasantest of all;—
I've Broom-seeds from a heathy glen,
    And ferns from an old stone wall.

12

Of wall-flower slips and roots I've got
  So many, that I'm fain,
Dear as they are to me, to turn
  Many adrift again.

My ivy-plant from Tintern's braved
  Four winters' stormy weather ;
I've scraps, too, from proud Kenilworth,
  And here they grow together.

The feathery seeds of clematis
  In Goodrich I have caught ;
Hartstongue from Ragland's lofty keep,
  With maiden-hair, I brought.

And so at Claremont, where the crowd
  Of rhododendrons grew,
My whims were humoured, and I now
  Am rearing one or two.

And e'en those little things can bring
  Before me, passing well,
The very nook where the scented leaves
  Of the graceful calamus dwell.
                  Louisa A. Twamley.

Broom....*Humility.*

THOMAS MILLER thus speaks of the "bonny Broom," in his Romance of Nature:—

Beautiful art thou, O Broom! waving in all thy rich array of green and gold, on the breezy bosom of the bee-haunted heath. The sleeping sunshine, and the silver-footed showers, the clouds that for ever play about the face of Heaven, the homeless winds, and the crystal-globed dews, that settle upon thy blossoms like sleep on the veined eyelids of an infant, are ever beating above and around thee, as if to tell that they rejoice in thy companionship, and that, although a thousand years have strided by with silent steps, time hath not abated an atom of their love. Who can tell the thoughts of Saxon Alfred when, wandering alone, crownless and sceptreless, he stretched himself on the lonely moor beneath the shadow of thy golden blossoms, sighing for the fair queen he had left far behind? When he bowed his kingly head, and, musing on thy beauty, buried in a solitary wild, thought how even regal dignity would be enhanced by humility, and that, although thou didst grow there unmarked and unpruned, not a more princely flower waved in his own English garden.

Humility, that low, sweet root,
From which all heavenly virtues shoot.

Moore.

Oh the Broom, the bonny bonny Broom,
   The Broom of the Cowden-knowes;
For sure so soft, so sweet a bloom,
   Elsewhere there never grows.
                      Scottish Song.

Here is a precious jewel I have found
Among the filth and rubbish of the world.
I'll stoop for it, but when I wear it here,
Set on my forehead like the morning-star,
The world may wonder, but it will not laugh.
                      Longfellow.

Their groves of sweet myrtle, let foreign lands reckon,
   Where bright beaming summers exalt the perfume;
Far dearer to me yon lone glen o' green breckan,
   Wi' the burn stealing under the lang yellow Broom.
                      Burns.

But the publican stood afar off in his grief,
For he felt like a beggar who needed relief;
And he raised not his eyes, and he saw not the scorn
Which the lip of the Pharisee proudly had worn.
But he smote on his bosom, and deeply he sighed;
As a sinner, for mercy, sweet mercy, he cried.
It was all he could utter, but GOD hears a sigh,
And listens, no matter how feeble the cry.
Both unheard and unblest, the proud Pharisee then
Returned to the pomp of his riches again;
While the publican sinner, though loathed and oppressed,
Went joyfully homeward with peace in his breast.
                      MacKellar.

St. John's Wort....*Superstition.*

THIS plant is an appropriate emblem of superstition; for it has always been regarded with reverence by the peasantry of Europe, on account of its real and supposed virtues. It was supposed to possess the power of defending persons from phantoms and spectres, and driving away all evil spirits. Its large, yellow flower grows close to the earth, and resembles a small wheel of fireworks.

'Tis a history
Handed from ages down; a nurse's tale—
Which children, open-eyed and mouthed, devour;
And thus as garrulous ignorance relates,
We learn it and believe.
Southey.

A fortune-telling host,
As numerous as the stars could boast,
Matrons, who toss the cup, and see
The grounds of fate in grounds of tea.
Churchill.

Gipsies, who every ill can cure,
Except the ill of being poor,
Who charms 'gainst love and agues sell,
Who can in hen-roost set a spell,

Prepared by arts, to them best known,
To catch all feet except their own,
Who as to fortune can unlock it,
As easily as pick a pocket.

Churchill.

We may smile, or coldly sneer,
The while such ghostly tales we hear,—
And wonder why they were believed,
And how wise men could be deceived:—
Bathing our renovated sight
In the free gospel's glorious light,
We marvel it was ever night!

Mrs. Hale.

This present life seems full of mysteries;
 The vulgar mind, to superstition prone,
In nature's workings fearful omens sees,
 And shrinks aghast from terrors of its own
Absurd imagining. Despotic is the power
 Of ignorance; and thousands live in fear
And die unnumbered times before the hour
 That Heaven has set to end their being here.
The trustful, quiet, mighty thinker seeks
 The beautiful and simple orderings
 Of the Great Former of created things,
And God to him in guiding accents speaks.
 Still, in the dealings of the Lord with men,
 Some things there are beyond our human ken.

MacKellar.

Tam saw an unco sight!
Warlocks and witches in a dance;
Nae cotillon brent new frae France,
But hornpipes, jigs, strathspeys, and reels,
Put life an mettle in their heels.
A winnock bunker in the east,
There sat auld Nick, in shape o' beast;
A towzie tyke, black, grim, and large,
To gie them music was his charge:
He screw'd the pipes and gart them skirl,
Till roof and rafters a' did dirl.—
Coffins stood round like open presses,
That shaw'd the dead in their last dresses;
And by some devilish cantraip slight,
Each in its cauld hand held a light,—
By which heroic Tam was able
To note upon the haly table,
A murderer's banes in gibbet airns;
Twa span-lang, wee, unchristen'd bairns;
A thief, new cutted frae a rape,
Wi' his last gasp his gab did gape;
Five tomahawks, wi' bluid red-rusted;
Five scimiters, wi' murder crusted;
A garter, which a babe had strangled;
A knife, a father's throat had mangled,
Whom his ain son o' life bereft,
The gray hairs yet stack to the heft;
Wi' mair o' horrible and awfu',
Which ev'n to name wad be unlawfu'.

Burns.

VERVAIN....*Enchantment.*

VERVAIN was employed by the ancients in various kinds of divinations. They ascribed to it a thousand properties, and, among others, that of reconciling enemies. Whenever the Romans sent their heralds to offer peace or war to nations, one of them always carried a sprig of Vervain. The Druids, both in Gaul and Britain, regarded the Vervain with the same veneration as the misletoe, and offered sacrifices to the earth before they cut this plant in spring, which was a ceremony of great pomp. Though the Druids and their religion have passed away, the Vervain is still the plant of spells and enchantment. In the northern provinces of France, the shepherds gather it with ceremonies and words known only to themselves, and express its juices under certain phases of the moon. They insist that this plant enables them to cure their ailments, and to cast a spell on their daughters and cattle, by which they can make them conform to their wishes.

> I'd wake the spell that sleeps within an herb,
> And witch the lady till I know she's mine.
> *Peerbold.*

> Her overpowering presence made you feel
> It would not be idolatry to kneel.
> *Byron.*

Her sacred beauty hath enchanted heaven,
And, had she lived before the siege of Troy,
Helen, whose beauty summoned Greece to arms,
And drew a thousand ships to Tenedos,
Had not been named in Homer's Iliad;
Her name had been in every line he wrote.

Marlowe.

Not all the charms that superstition gave
To plants in lonely forests found,
Could work such magic in Love's doting slave,
As the voice which his wishes crowned.

Anon.

A voice of laughter—a voice of glee!
Among the maidens, who happy as she?
By love's enchantment her thrilling breast
Is wildly, witchingly, over-blest:
And gushing joys, like the sun in May,
Enliven the noon of her bridal-day.

MacKellar.

Mysterious plant! whose golden tresses wave
With a sad beauty in the dying year,
Blooming amid November's frost severe,
Like a pale corpse-light o'er the recent grave.
If shepherds tell us true, thy wand hath power,
With gracious influence, to avert the harm
Of ominous planets.

Token, 1831.

Corn....*Riches.*

CERES, the goddess of Corn and harvest, was represented with a garland of ears of Corn on her head. The commemoration of the loss of her daughter Proserpine, was celebrated about the beginning of harvest; that of her search after her, at the time of sowing Corn. A whole straw has been made the emblem of union; and a broken straw, of rupture. The custom of breaking a straw, to express the rupture of a contract, may be traced back to an early period of French history, and may be said to have had a royal origin. When Charles the Simple, of France, was abandoned by his principal lords, they broke a straw to express that they would no longer acknowledge him as their king. Corn may be regarded as an appropriate emblem of wealth; since, wherever it grows, it leads us to infer plenty and comfort.

> Therefore, if at great things thou wouldst arrive,
> Get riches first, get wealth.
>
> *Milton.*

> Then let us get money, like bees lay up honey;
> We'll build us new hives and store each cell;
> The sight of our treasure shall yield us great pleasure,
> We'll count it, and chink it, and jingle it well.
>
> *Dr. Franklin.*

Much learning shows how little mortals know;
Much wealth, how little worldlings can enjoy:
At best, it babies us with endless toys,
And keeps us children till we drop to dust.
As monkeys at a mirror stand amazed,
They fail to find what they so plainly see;
Thus men, in shining riches, see the face
Of happiness, nor know it as a shade;
But gaze, and touch, and peep, and peep again,
And wish, and wonder it is absent still.

Young.

Oh, blessed lot

To be possessed of wealth and of a heart
So heavenly made that it refuses not
Of its abundance freely to impart!

MacKellar.

You are heir

To lordships, mansions, forests, parks, and gems.
You have three mighty manors in Castile;
Two broad estates in Leon; two amidst
The mulberry trees of Murcia, and huge chests
Crammed full of ingots, dug by naked slaves,
Who famished on coarse bread. Besides all these,
There bloom plantations in the East, whose fruits
Are pearls, and spice, and princely diamonds;
And in Brazil, Pactolus floods, ne'er dumb,
Whose waves all talk in gold!

Barry Cornwall.

CRANBERRY....*Cure for the Heartache.*

FAR away among the hills,
  Far from tower and town,
Where wide moors and heaths lie spread,
  Desolate and brown.

Where the grouse and plover live
  Far from gun and dog,
A delicate and tiny flower
  Decks swamp and watery bog.

The Cranberry blossom dwelleth there
  Amid the mountains cold,
Seeming like a fairy gift
  Left on the dreary wold.

Oh! and 'tis very beautiful,
  The flowers are pink and white,
And the small oval polished leaves
  Are evergreen and bright.

'Tis such a wee, fair, dainty thing,
  You'd think a greenhouse warm
Would be its proper dwelling-place,
  Kept close from wind and storm.

But on the moors it dwelleth free,
  Like a fearless mountain child;

With a rosy cheek, a lightsome look,
  And a spirit strong and wild.

In autumn, all among the swamps
  And marshes soft and wet,
Come troops of poor hill-children
  The ripened fruit to get.

The bushes all in water grow,
  In those small pools, that lie
In scores among the turfy knolls
  On mountains broad and high.

And there the peasant children come
  To pull the Cranberries red,
Where bold and booted sporting squires
  Would scarcely dare to tread.

They only shoot the poor wild birds,
  And chase the timid hare,
For their diversion; *they* can live
  In luxury, without care.

But these poor peasant-children's lot
  Is full of human wo,
And hungry, thinly clad, and cold,
  They o'er the mountains go;

With feet, that shoes have never known,
  And legs all blue and bare,
And yet, so light are they of heart,
  You'll hear them laughing there.

Such laughter makes my very heart
  Leap up with joy to hear,
It tells that even poverty
  Is not entirely drear.

It telleth—what I ever think,
  That God is good indeed;
And that he suiteth, in us all,
  Our spirit to our need.

Think ye—if these poor peasants were
  All discontent and sour—
If they in frowns and murmurings
  Spent every wretched hour:—

Like many a cherished, pampered child,
  Whom wealth and fondness cloy,
Till e'en the knowledge of a want
  Would be a novel joy:—

Think, if these peasants pined like him
  For pleasures they have not,
How manifold would then have been
  The sorrows of their lot!

But they, unshod, bareheaded too,
  Fed sparsely with coarse food,
Go laughing on their gleesome way,
  As God's bright creatures should.

They are like flowers, springing up
  In some unkindly place,

Yet full of all their colours rare,·
  Their sweetness and their grace.

They *are* bright flowers, that spring to cheer
  E'en penury's wilderness,
And often with a swelling heart,
  Those human flowers I bless.

Kind blessings on their bold, clear eyes,
  And elvish, unbound hair ;—
And blessings on their laughter wild,
  Mid crags and moorlands bare!

In autumn mornings forth they go
  With baskets to the wold,
Some of wicker, some of rush,
  Some new, and many old.

And over mountain, over glen,
  The merry creatures bound,
On to the wide and boggy heaths,
  Where a thousand streamlets sound.

The small bare legs all splash about,
  Heeding not cold nor wet,
So long as busy eyes can see,
  And hands the treasure get.

"*And after all this toil and moil,*
  What profit win they thence?"—
Perhaps a long day's work may bring
  A few poor sordid pence.

But more than hundreds to the rich
  Are pennies to the poor,
And thankfully they seek and sell
  The Cranberries on the moor.
                  Louisa A. Twamley.

The heart of kindness seldom sours or curdles;
The cream of love is in it pure and sweet:
With every charm that human nature girdles,
And every grace of gentleness replete,
The man who has a kindly heart is most
In pattern like his LORD; for where the law
Of kindness rules the heart, the virtues draw
Together in companionship, and post
Themselves around that citadel of love.
The kindly man doth always kindly prove:
He has a word of sweetness for the child—
Of pity for the poor—of sympathy
For all who mourn; and truly glad is he
When through his generous care some sorrowing face
      has smiled.
There's music ever in the kindly soul,
For every deed of goodness done is like
A chord set in the heart, and joy doth strike
Upon it oft as memory doth unroll
The immortal page whereon good deeds are writ;
And Heaven gives nothing sweeter to the mind
Than memories of the acts that bless our human kind.
                  MacKellar.

IVY.... *Constancy.*

IN Greece the altar of Hymen was enwreathed with
Ivy, and a branch of it was presented to the new-married couple, as a symbol of the indissoluble knot. It
was sacred to Bacchus, who is represented crowned
with Ivy leaves, as well as those of the vine. It formed
the crown of the Greek and Roman poets; and, in modern times, has been made the poet's frequent image
of constancy. The Ivy is attached to the earth by its
own roots, and derives no nourishment from the sub-
stances to which it clings. The protector of ruins, it
adorns the dilapidated walls which it holds together;
it will not accept every kind of support, but its attachment ends only with its life.

When all things have their trial, you shall find
Nothing is constant but a virtuous mind.
Shirley.

The mountain rill
Seeks with no surer flow the far, bright sea,
Than my unchanged affections flow to thee.
Park Benjamin.

I am constant as the northern star;
Of whose true, fixed, and resting quality
There is no fellow in the firmament.
Shakspeare.

12

Make my breast
Transparent as pure crystal, that the world,
Jealous of me, may see the foulest thought
My heart does hold.   Where shall a woman turn
Her eyes to find out constancy?

Buckingham.

No, never from this hour to part,
    We'll live and love so true,
The sigh that rends thy constant heart,
    Shall break thy Edwin's too.

Goldsmith.

The Ivy round some lofty pile
    Its twining tendril flings;
Though fled from thence be pleasure's smile,
    It yet the fonder clings;
As lonelier still becomes the place,
The warmer is its fond embrace,
    More firm its verdant rings;
As if it loved its shade to rear
O'er one devoted to despair.
Thus shall my bosom cling to thine,
    Unchanged by gliding years;
Through Fortune's rise, or her decline,
    In sunshine, or in tears;
And though between us oceans roll,
And rocks divide us, still my soul
    Shall feel no jealous fears:
Confiding in a heart like thine,
Love's uncontaminated shrine.

Mrs. Hale.

HOLLY....*Foresight.*

THE Holly, with its scarlet berries, is the most beautiful of the evergreens that have been used for ages to adorn the churches of old England, during the Christmas season. It is an ornament to the woods, stripped bare by the rude breath of winter; its berries serve for food for the little birds that never leave us, and its foliage affords them an hospitable shelter during the cold season. Nature, by a seeming forethought, has been careful to preserve the verdure of this handsome tree all the year round, and to arm it with thorns, that it may furnish both food and protection to the innocent creatures which resort to it for shelter. It may be added, however, that from the bark of the common Holly, when fermented and washed from the woody fibres, is made the bird-lime which is used for catching small birds.

With Holly and ivy,
   So green and so gay,
We deck up our houses
   As fresh as the day;
With bays and rosemary,
   And laurel complete,
And every one now
   Is a king in conceit.
         Poor Robin's Almanac, 1695.

THE HOLLY TREE.

O Reader! hast thou ever stood to see
　　The Holly tree?
The eye that contemplates it well perceives
　　Its glossy leaves,
Ordered by an intelligence so wise
As might confound the atheist's sophistries.

Below, a circling fence its leaves are seen,
　　Wrinkled and keen;
No grazing cattle, through their prickly round
　　Can reach to wound;
But as they grow where nothing is to fear,
Smooth and unarmed the pointless leaves appear.

I love to view these things with curious eyes
　　And moralize;
And in this wisdom of the Holly tree
　　Can emblems see,
Wherewith, perchance, to make a pleasant rhyme,
One which may profit in the after-time.

Thus, though abroad, perchance I might appear
　　Harsh and austere,
To those who on my leisure would intrude
　　Reserved and rude,
Gentle at home amid my friends I'd be,
Like the high leaves upon the Holly tree.

And should my youth, as youth is apt, I know,
　　Some harshness show,

All vain asperities I day by day
    Would wear away,
Till the smooth temper of my age should be
Like the high leaves upon the Holly tree.

And as when all the summer trees are seen
    So bright and green,
The Holly leaves a sober hue display,
    Less bright than they;
But when the bare and wintry woods we see,
What then so cheerful as the Holly tree?

So serious should my youth appear among
    The thoughtless throng,
So would I seem amid the young and gay
    More grave than they,
That in my age as cheerful I might be
As the green winter of the Holly tree.

        Southey.

To know the road ere on't we trust the foot,
And where it leads, and what, while journeying,
We may meet, is Wisdom's eager wish.

        Peerbold.

Walk
Boldly and wisely in that light thou hast;
There is a hand above will help thee on.

        Bailey.

MEADOW SAFFRON.....*My best days are past.*

THE Meadow Saffron, or Colchicum Autumnale, springs up about the time the leaves begin to fall from the trees, and may, therefore, be said to proclaim to all nature, that the bright days of summer are past. According to Ovid, this autumnal flower owes its origin to some drops of the magic liquor prepared by Medea, to restore the aged Æson to the bloom and vigour of youth, which were spilled in the fields. As a medicine, the Colchicum is powerful, but dangerous, and must be used with caution. The poisonous quality of the plant seems to be known, as if by instinct, to all kinds of cattle. They all shun it, and in many pastures this alone will be found standing, when all other herbage has been consumed.

> Why grieve that time has brought so soon
>   The sober age of manhood on?
> As idly should I weep at noon
>   To see the blush of morning gone.
> True, time will sear and blanch my brow:
>   Well—I shall sit with aged men,
> And my good glass will tell me how
>   A grisly beard becomes me then.
> And should no foul dishonour lie
>   Upon my head when I am gray,
> Love yet may search my fading eye,
>   And smooth the path of my decay.
>   *Bryant.*

SWEET PEA   PANSY

I depart   Think on me

Oh! thou who dry'st the mourner's tear,
   How dark this world would be,
If, when deceived and wounded here,
   We could not fly to thee!
The friends who in our sunshine live,
   When winter comes, are flown;
And he who has but tears to give,
   Must weep those tears alone:
But thou wilt heal that broken heart,
   Which, like the plants that throw
Their fragrance from the wounded part,
   Breathes sweetness out of wo.

Moore.

Then bright from earth, amid the troubled sky,
Ascends fair Colchicum, with radiant eye,
Warms the cold bosom of the hoary year,
And lights with beauty's blaze the dusky sphere.

Darwin.

The world around me groweth gray and old:
   My friends are dropping one by one away;
   Some live in distant lands—some in the clay
Rest quietly, their mortal moments told.
   And when my children gather at my knee
To worship God and sing our morning psalm,
   Their rising stature whispers unto me
My life is waning towards its evening calm.

MacKellar.

China Aster.... *Variety.*

The China Aster. begins to blow when other flowers
are scarce. It is like an afterthought of Flora's, who
smiles at leaving us. The China Aster was introduced
into Europe by Father d'Insarville, a Jesuit missionary;
who, about the year 1730, sent seeds of it to the royal
gardens of Paris. As, by cultivation, many varieties
of the Aster have been obtained, the flower has been
made the emblem of variety.

The sleepless streams move onward
Through beds of idling lilies,
Chiding the foolish flowers
That watch their mirrored beauty;
So live the thoughtless many,
Who throng the halls of fashion.

Dawes.

I love the ever-varying hue
  Upon the face of heaven;
I would not have it always blue,
  But oft with lightning riven.
I would not have wide oceans spread
  A mirror e'er to see;
But lashed to many a cresty head
  By scowling tempests free!

C. Watson.

Play every string in love's sweet lyre—
  Set all its music flowing;
Be air, and dew, and light, and fire,
  To keep the soul-flower growing.
                              Mrs. Osgood.

The rapid and the deep—the fall, the gulf,
Have likenesses in feeling and in life.
And life, so varied, hath more loveliness
In one day than a creeping century
Of sameness.
                              Bailey.

      Youth loves and lives on change,
Till the soul sighs for sameness; which at last
Becomes variety; and takes its place.
                              Bailey.

Variety's the source of joy below,
From which still fresh revolving pleasures flow;
In books and love the mind one end pursues,
And only change the expiring flame renews.
                              Gay.

Wherefore did nature pour her bounties forth
With such a full and unwithdrawing hand,
Covering the earth with odours, fruits, and flocks,
Thronging the seas with spawn innumerable,
But all to please and sate a curious taste?
                              Milton.

American Starwort.... *Welcome.*

The Starwort is another late-blooming flower. It is exclusively indigenous to North America and the Cape of Good Hope. The flowers are of every variety of hue, and present a very attractive appearance.

Stranger, new flowers in our vales are seen,
With a dazzling eye, and a lovely green.—
They scent the breath of the dewy morn:
They feed no worm, and they hide no thorn,
But revel and grow in our balmy air;
They are flowers which Freedom hath planted there.

This bud of welcome to thee we give,—
Bid its unborn sweets in thy bosom live;
It shall charm thee from all a stranger's pain,
Reserve, suspicion, and dark disdain:
A race in its freshness and bloom are we;
Bring no cares from a worn-out world with thee.

      Mrs. Sigourney.

JUNIPER....*Protection.*

THE Juniper has been the favourite of Superstition. The ancients consecrated the shrub to the Furies. The smoke of its green roots was the incense which they offered in preference to the infernal gods; and they burned its berries during funerals to ban malign influences. In some parts of Europe, the peasant still believes that the perfume of Juniper berries purifies the air, and drives evil spirits from his humble cot. The Juniper is made to signify protection, on account of the defensive qualities ascribed to it by superstition, and the shelter its drooping branches afford to small animals which are hard pressed by the hunters.

I have found out a gift for my fair;
  I have found where the wood-pigeons breed;
But let me that plunder forbear,
  She will say, 'twas a barbarous deed.

"For he ne'er could be true," she averred,
  "Who could rob a poor bird of its young;"
And I loved her the more, when I heard
  Such tenderness fall from her tongue.

                                          Shenstone.

Hazel....*Peace—Reconciliation.*

Fable gives the following account of the origin of the signification of the Hazel. There was a time when men were at constant war with each other, and could not be restrained from cruelty and revenge by any tie of kin. The gods at length took pity on them. Apollo and Mercury made presents to each other, and descended to the earth. The god of harmony received from the son of Maia the shell of a tortoise, out of which he had constructed a lyre, and gave him in exchange a Hazel stick, which had the power of imparting a love of virtue and of reconciling hearts divided by envy and hate. By the power thus given him, Mercury taught men the love of peace, and of home and country, and made commerce the bond of nations. Adorned with two light wings, and entwined with serpents, the Hazel rod given to the god of eloquence by the god of harmony is still, by the name of caduceus, the emblem of peace, commerce, and reconciliation.

Oh then that wisdom may we know,
Which leads a life of peace below!

Sprague.

Peace, sweet peace is ever found
In her eternal home on holy ground.

Mrs. Embury.

And see,
As yet unclothed, the Hazel tree
Prepares his early tufts to lend
The coppice first-fruits ; and depend
In russet drops, whose clustered rows,
Still closed in part, in part disclose,
Yet fenced beneath their scaly shed,
The pendent anther's yellow head.

Louisa A. Twamley.

I trust the frown thy features wear,
　Ere long into a smile will turn ;
I would not that a face as fair
　As thine, beloved, should look so stern.
The chain of ice that winter binds,
　Holds not for aye the sparkling rill ;
It melts away when summer shines,
　And leaves the waters sparkling still :
Thus let thy cheek resume the smile
　That shed such sunny light before ;
And though I left thee for a while,
　I'll vow to leave thee, love, no more.

Wm. Leggett.

Come, while the morning of thy life is glowing,
　Ere the dim phantoms thou art chasing die—
Ere the gay spell, which earth is round thee throwing,
　Fades like the crimson from a sunset sky.
Life is but shadows, save a promise given,
　Which lights up sorrow with a fadeless ray.
Oh, touch the sceptre !—with a hope in heaven,
　Come, turn thy spirit from the world away.

Anon.

18

Oak....*Nobility.*

THE form of the Oak tree, when grown fairly and naturally, is a perfect emblem of its qualities, so firm set, so massive, and strong. You may always know it instantly, whether as a wintry skeleton form, bare, and gnarled, and angular, or in its summer garb of rich and finely massed foliage, always the monarch of the woods.

> True is, that whilome that good poet said,
> The gentle mind by gentle deeds is known,
> For man by nothing is so well bewrayed
> As by his manners, in which plain is shown
> Of what degree and what race he is grown.
>
> *Spenser.*

> How vain are all hereditary honours,
> Those poor possessions from another's deeds,
> Unless our own just virtues form our title,
> And give a sanction to our fond assumption!
>
> *Shirley.*

>   Whoe'er amidst the sons
> Of reason, valour, liberty, and virtue,
> Displays distinguished merit, is a noble
> Of nature's own creating. Such have risen,
> Sprung from the dust; or where had been our honours?
>
> *Thomson.*

LIFE OF AN OAK TREE.

Long centuries have come and passed
   Since, in a stormy wind,
An acorn fell one autumn day,
   Like thousands of his kind.

The wild swine fed in the forests then,
   And hungry beasts were they;
They crunched the mast where'er it fell,
   And they feasted well that day.

But as they trampled all about
   With heavy hoofs, they trod
That acorn—perchance hundreds more—
   Deep in the yielding sod.

Years came and went.—The acorn grew
   And became a young Oak tree;
With a slender, straight, and flexile stem,
   Dressed in rich greenery.

Time passeth on.—The young tree rose
   A bold and noble thing;
Each summer showed a leafier crest,
   And a longer shoot each spring.

There came into the ancient wood
   Some stern official men;
They marked the fairest, loftiest trees,
   And they were doomèd then.

They glanced upon the tall young Oak,
  And quickly passed it by,
And laughing harshly, said 'twould do
  By the next century.

Soon through the forest's solemn glades
  There rang that deathful sound,
The woodman's axe ;—and crashing fell
  Trunks, branches, all around.

Craftsmen of many kinds there came
  For that oak timber good,
And carried it in loads away
  From its old native wood.

Some floated far o'er ocean's waves
  Mid stormy winds and squalls,
Both merchant-ships, and men-of-war,
  "Old England's Wooden Walls."

Some, raised on high, with rare device
  The royal roof support,
And look down in the banquet-hall
  On king, and queen, and court.

Some, quaintly carved, and polished fair,
  May shrine a pictured face,
Of Dolci's gentle loveliness,
  Or Raphael's angel grace.

And many a toilet mirror owes,
  Its flowered and gilded frame

To the good trees of which I sing:—
  Well have they won their fame!

And massive tables, that have once
  Groaned·'neath baronial fare,
If they could talk of that Oak wood,
  Might tell of dwelling there.—

The young Oak tree yet statelier grew,
  And broader spread its shade,
And the dappled deer lay sheltered 'neath
  The canopy it made.

Years came and went.—The Oak tree stood
  In full-grown prime and pride,
And lords of various mind and mood
  Possessed those woodlands wide.

The first, a reckless forester,
  Loved horse, and hawk, and hound,
And he chased all o'er his wide domains,
  Wellnigh the whole year round.

His lady fair, as dames were wont,
  In those long bygone days,
Loved hawking too; and gallant trains
  She led through forest ways.

'Twas a merry and a winsome thing,
  When lord, and squire, and knight
Rode forth, mid bugles ringing shrill,
  With dainty ladies bright,

14

To sweep along by vale and hill,
　Or through the forest glade,
Where the echoes of their laughter light
　A merry music made.

And oft they reined their palfreys in
　Beneath the young Oak tree,
And oft foretold how grand a thing
　In after-time 'twould be.

These jocund sports passed all away;
　For direful civil war
Spread its fell curse throughout the land,
　Wasting it near and far.

And the next lord these broad lands had,
　A warrior stern was he,
He dwelt with camps and cannon more
　Than sylvan glade and tree.

He died in battle ; and his lands
　By craft and deeds unfair,
His brother claimed and won, although
　His infant son was heir.

This hard, bad man was miserly,
　And loved no thing save gold ;
He soon marked out the stately tree,
　To be cut down and sold.

What was its beauty unto him ?—
　The grand and noble thing !

His dull eyes only measured well
　　What moneys it would bring.

But while he doomed the lordly oak,
　　His wicked life ebbed low,
And suddenly, death summoned him
　　From his ill-got hoards to go.

The grand estate—the ancient hall,
　　The woods, and wealth untold,
Came then unto that warrior's child,
　　A boy of ten years old.

He was a thoughtful, quiet boy,
　　For though yet young in years,
His mother's sorrows and his own
　　Had made him old in tears.

And with a calm and gentle joy
　　Came home that youthful heir,
For his chief source of gladness was,
　　To bring his mother there:—

To watch her sadly smile to see
　　Again each well-known spot,
Where days of happiness had passed,
　　That ne'er could be forgot:—

To have her former state restored,
　　Maidens, and serving-men ;
And garments, richer than of old,
　　He bade them bring her then.

The gardens, that the miser had
  Left all untrimmed and bare,
Were planted, pruned, and decked anew,
  And stored with all things rare.

But chiefly did the lady love
  One glade within the wood,
The shady glade, where broad and high,
  The noble Oak tree stood.

Sad memories, yet sweet ones too,
  For her that lone spot bore:
'Twas there she parted from her lord
  To meet on earth no more!

'Twas there, beneath that tree, he spoke
  His last, *last* fond farewell!
From thence she watched him ride away
  The eve before he fell:—
No marvel that sad lady loved
  The silent spot so well!

And there they oft together came,
  The lady and the boy,
For he to her was all on earth,
  Her one sole living joy.

And long years after, when she slept
  Her warrior's tomb beside,
When the boy had grown an aged man,
  With grandsons by his side:—

That ancient wood he reverenced;
  And peasants, when they spoke

Of the old tree within the glade,
  Called it—the Lady's Oak.

I know the spot—though strangely time
  Hath altered all around,
Where once the forest's stillness lay,
  Now whirling wheels resound.

A large and busy peopled town
  E'en on that spot we see,
Where dappled deer and timid birds
  Dwelt fearlessly and free.

But I remember when a child,
  One old and mouldering shell
Of a most ancient, huge Oak tree
  Stood near the public well.

I've sat within it many a time,
  In childish sport and play,
And much I mourned to see at last
  The trunk quite cleared away.

Soon they built there a fine new street,
  And noisy coaches sweep
With roar and riot,—even where
  That lady came to weep!

Each passing year we note a change
  In ancient things and new;
And if we see so much in one,
  What may not hundreds do?

                    Louisa A. Twamley.

There's no power
In ancestry, to make the foolish wise,
The ignorant learned, the cowardly and base
Deserving our respect as brave and good.
All men feel this: nor dares the despot say
His fiat can endow with truth the soul,
Or, like a pension, on the heart bestow
The virtues current in the realms above.
Hence man's best riches must be gained—not given;
His noblest name deserved, and not derived.

Mrs. Hale.

Some men are born to endure the toil and strife
    And heavy burdens of the earth.   They are
The pillars in the temple of this life,
    Its strength and ornament; or, hidden far
Beneath, they form its firm foundation-stone.
In nobleness they stand distinct and lone,
    Yet other men upon them lean, and fain
(Such selfishness in human bosoms swells)
    Would lay on them the weight of their own pain.
Where greatness is, a patient spirit dwells;
    They least repine who bear and suffer most:
In still and stern endurance they sustain
The ills whereof all weaker minds complain;
    And in their blessed lot they stand, without a sigh
        or boast.

MacKellar.

Yew....*Sorrow.*

THE Yew is among all nations an emblem of sorrow. Its bare trunk, and dark foliage, with which its fruit, looking like drops of blood, stands in harsh contrast, excite in us a sort of aversion. Persons who sleep under a Yew tree are liable to be seized with dizziness, heaviness, and violent headache. Its juice is poisonous, and the tree exhausts the soil which supports it, and destroys all other plants which spring up beneath it. The Yew was planted in old English burying-grounds, and its wood was commonly employed for making bows and arrows before the introduction of fire-arms. The Greeks, impressed with the melancholy aspect of this tree, invented the fable of the unhappy Smilax; who, seeing that her love was rejected by young Crocus, was transformed into a Yew.

> Who that hath ever been,
>   Could bear to be no more?
> Yet who would tread again the scene
>   He trod through life before?
>
> *Montgomery.*

> Griefs of mine own lie heavy in my breast;
> Which thou wilt propagate, to have them prest
> With more of thine: this love, that thou hast shown,
> Doth add more grief to too much of mine own.
>
> *Shakspeare.*

And sorrowing friends stood round the bed
   Whereon a form was lying:
'Twas Ellen;—there the suffering saint,
Without a murmur or complaint,
   In peace and hope was dying.
A silence deep as death was there
   When her true soul departed;
And grace and mercy crowned her end
   Who lived the broken-hearted.
                    MacKellar.

When the cold breath of sorrow is sweeping
   O'er the chords of the youthful heart,
And the earnest eye, dimmed with strange weeping,
   Sees the visions of fancy depart;
When the bloom of young feeling is dying,
   And the heart throbs with passion's fierce strife
When our sad days are wasted in sighing,
   Who then can find sweetness in life?
                    Mrs. Embury.

He is dead. Those words toll on the ear,
The knell of hopes, and fears, and fleshy aims.
The spirit light has cast a farewell beam—
Has shaken off its way-worn gear, and winged
To heaven. Sorrow will demand her tears,
For he was lovely, and leaves a hollow
In our near-drawn sphere which none may upclose.
But thoughts of heaven, through tears, will light us,
Making that refresh which seemed to blast!
                    C. Watson.

DEAD LEAVES....*Death.*

A MORE appropriate emblem of death than the remains of the forest's refreshing verdure could not be
selected. Withered by the chill breath of ruthless
Winter, the leaves strew the earth; and, in time, mingle with the dust, like ourselves. The eye cannot help
watching how the winds pursue, scatter, whirl, and
drive these remnants of departed life.

No longer mourn for me when I am dead.
　　Then you shall hear the surly, sullen bell
Give warning to the world that I am fled
　　From this vile world, with vilest worms to dwell.
Nay, if you read this line, remember not
　　The hand that writ it, for I love you so,
That I in your sweet thoughts would be forgot,
　　If thinking of me then should work you wo!
　　　　　　　　　　　　　　Shakspeare.

Now shall my verse, which thou in life didst grace,
Not leave thee in the grave, that ugly place,
That few regard, or have respect unto:
Where all attendance and observance ends;
Where all the sunshine of our favour sets;
Where what was ill no countenance defends,
And what was good the unthankful world forgets.
　　　　　　　　　　　　　　Daniel.

Hence, profane grim man ! nor dare
To approach so neere my faire.
Marble vaults, and gloomy caves,
Church-yards, charnell-houses, graves,
Where the living loath to be,
Heaven hath designed to thee.
But if needs 'mongst us thou'lt rage,
Let thy fury feed on age.

Habington.

So doth the swiftly turning wheel not stand
I' the instant we withdraw the moving hand,
But some short time retains a faint, weak course,
By virtue of the first impulsive force ;
And so, whilst I cast on thy funeral pile
Thy crown of bays, oh let it crack awhile,
And spit disdain, till the devouring flashes
Suck all the moisture up, then turn to ashes.

Carew.

Ah ! thou hast left to live ; and in the time
When scarce thou blossom'dst in thy pleasant prime:
So falls by northern blast a virgin rose,
At half that doth her bashful bosom close ;
So a sweet flower languishing decays,
That late did blush when kissed by Phœbus' rays;
So Phœbus mounting the meridian's height,
Choked by pale Phœbe, faints unto our sight;
Astonished Nature sullen stands to see
The life of all this all so changed to be ;
In gloomy gowns the stars this loss deplore,
The sea with murmuring mountains beats the shore.

Drummond.

Death is the crown of life:
Were death denied, poor men would live in vain;
Were death denied, to live would not be life:
Were death denied, even fools would wish to die.

Young.

Death is the sea, and we like rivers flow
To lose our selves in the insatiate maine,
Whence rivers may, she ne'er returne againe.
Nor grieve this christall streame so soone did fall
Into the ocean; since shee perfumed all
The banks she past, so that each neighbour field
Did sweete flowers cherish by her watring, yeeld,
Which now adorne her herse.

Habington.

We bore him to the grave while yet 'twas morn,
   The winter sunlight shining on his coffin:
The weight of grief was heavy to be borne,
   And the salt tears rose in our eyelids often.
We slowly walked in mutely sad procession;
   The pitying people freely made us way;
And the blest child, yet guiltless of transgression,
   We softly placed between the walls of clay.
   We sang a hymn—we bowed our heads to pray;
And God, who had our bitter grief appointed,
Sent also strengthening grace by lips anointed.
   We looked again on George as low he lay
Deep in the earth; and when we homeward went,
We felt his home was better 'yond the firmament.

MacKellar.

MISTLETOE....*I climb to greatness.*

THE Mistletoe is a creeping plant which grows on the tops of the tallest trees. The proud oak is its slave, and nourishes it with his own substance. The Druids paid a kind of adoration to it, as the emblem of a weakness that was superior to strength: they regarded the tyrant of the oak as equally formidable to men and gods.

> 'Tis a common proof,
> That lowliness is young ambition's ladder,
> Whereto the climber upwards turns his face:
> But when he once attains the upmost round,
> He then unto the ladder turns his back,
> Looks in the clouds, scorning the base degrees
> By which he did ascend.
> > *Shakspeare.*

> He who ascends to mountain-tops shall find
>   The loftiest peaks most wrapt in clouds and snow;
> He who surpasses or subdues mankind
>   Must look down on the hate of those below.
> Though high above the sun of glory glow,
>   And far beneath the earth and ocean spread,
> Round him are icy rocks, and loudly blow
>   Contending tempests on his naked head,
> And thus reward the toils which to those summits led.
> > *Byron.*

Ye gods, it doth amaze me,
A man of such a feeble temper should
So get the start of the majestic world,
And bear the palm alone.

Shakspeare.

On the summit see,
The seals of office glitter in his eyes ;
He climbs,—he pants,—he grasps them. At his heels,
Close at his heels, a demagogue ascends,
And with a dexterous jerk soon twists him down;
And wins them, but to lose them in his turn.

Cowper.

If any man must fall for me to rise,
   Then seek I not to rise.   Another's pain
   I choose not for my good.   A golden chain—
A robe of honour is too poor a prize
   To tempt my hasty hand to do a wrong
Unto a fellow man.   This life hath wo
Sufficient, wrought by man's satanic foe ;
   And who that hath a heart would dare prolong
Or add unto the sorrows of a soul
That seeks some healing balm to make it whole ?
   My bosom owns the brotherhood of man ;
From God and truth a renegade is he
Who scorns a poor man in his poverty,
   Or on his fellow lays a supercilious ban.

MacKellar.

ASH TREE....*Grandeur.*

It is sure,
Stamped by the seal of nature, that the well
Of mind, where all its waters gather pure,
Shall with unquestioned spell all hearts allure.
Wisdom enshrined in beauty—Oh! how high
The order of that loveliness.

Percival.

The sky is changed!—and such a change! O night,
  And storm, and darkness, ye are wondrous strong,
Yet lovely in your strength, as is the light
  Of a dark eye in woman! Far along,
From peak to peak, the rattling crags among
  Leaps the live thunder! Not from one lone cloud,
But every mountain now hath found a tongue,
  And Jura answers, through her misty shroud,
Back to the joyous Alps, who call to her aloud!
And this is in the night:—most glorious night!
  Thou wert not sent for slumber! let me be
A sharer in thy fierce and far delight,—
  A portion of the tempest and of thee!
How the lit lake shines, a phosphoric sea,
  And the big rain comes dancing to the earth!
And now again 'tis black,—and now, the glee
  Of the loud hills shakes with its mountain mirth,
As if they did rejoice o'er a young earthquake's birth.

Byron.

I'll go along, no such sight to be shown,
But to rejoice in splendour of mine own.
Shakspeare.

But lo! the dome—the vast and wondrous dome,
   To which Diana's marvel was a cell—
Christ's mighty shrine above his martyr's tomb!
   I have beheld the Ephesian's miracle—
Its columns strew the wilderness, and dwell
   The hyæna and the jackal in their shade;
I have beheld Sophia's bright roofs swell
   Their glittering mass i' the sun, and have surveyed
Its sanctuary the while the usurping Moslem prayed;
   But thou, of temples old, or altars new,
   Standest alone—with nothing like to thee—
Worthiest of GOD, the holy and the true.
   Since Zion's desolation, when that He
Forsook his former city, what could be,
   Of earthly structures in his honour piled,
   Of a sublimer aspect? Majesty,
   Power, glory, strength, and beauty, all are aisled
In this eternal ark of worship undefiled.
   Enter: its grandeur overwhelms thee not;
   And why? it is not lessened; but thy mind,
Expanded by the genius of the spot,
   Has grown colossal, and can only find
A fit abode wherein appear enshrined
   Thy hopes of immortality; and thou
Shalt one day, if found worthy, so defined,
   See thy God face to face, as thou dost now
His Holy of Holies, nor be blasted by his brow.
                   Byron.

What peremptory, eagle-sighted eye
Dares look upon the heaven of her brow,
That is not blinded by her majesty?

Shakspeare.

The glorious sun
Stays in his course, and plays the alchymist,
Turning, with splendour of his precious eye,
The meagre, cloddy earth to glittering gold.

Shakspeare.

No! I shall never lose the trace,
Of what I've felt in this bright place;
And should my spirit's hope grow weak,—
Should I, O God! forget thy power,
This mighty scene again I'll seek,
At the same calm and glowing hour;
And here at the sublimest shrine
That nature ever reared to thee,
Rekindle all that hope divine,
And feel my immortality!

Moore.

CHAMOMILE....*Energy in Adversity.*

Italy!
Time, which hath wronged thee with ten thousand rents
Of thine imperial garment, shall deny,
And hath denied, to every other sky,
Spirits which soar from ruin:—thy decay
Is still impregnate with divinity.
Which gilds it with revivifying ray.

Byron.

I said to Penury's meagre train,
 Come on—your threats I brave;
My last poor life-drop you may drain,
 And crush me to the grave;
Yet still the spirit that endures,
 Shall mock your force the while,
And meet each cold, cold grasp of yours
 With bitter smile.

I said to cold Neglect and Scorn,
 Pass on—I heed you not;
Ye may pursue me till my form
 And being are forgot;
Yet still, the spirit which you see
 Undaunted by your wiles,
Draws from its own nobility
 Its high-born smiles.

Mrs. Hale.

15

When a great mind falls,
The noble nature of man's generous heart
Doth bear him up against the shame of ruin,
With gentle censure, using but his faults
As modest means to introduce his praise;
For pity, like a dewy twilight, comes
To close th' oppressive splendour of his day,
And they who but admired him in his height
His altered state lament, and love him fallen.
                                    Joanna Baillie.

Oh, more or less than man—in high or low,
  Battling with nations, flying from the field;
Now making monarchs' necks thy footstool, now
  More than thy meanest soldier taught to yield;
An empire thou couldst crush, command, rebuild,
  But govern not thy pettiest passion, nor,
However deeply in men's spirits skilled,
  Look through thine own, nor curb the lust of war,
Nor learn that tempted fate will leave the loftiest star.
Yet well thy soul hath brooked the turning tide
  With that untaught innate philosophy,
Which, be it wisdom, coldness, or deep pride,
  Is gall and wormwood to an enemy.
When the whole host of hatred stood hard by,
  To watch and mock thee shrinking, thou hast smiled
With a sedate and all-enduring eye;—
  When fortune fled her spoiled and favourite child,
He stood unbowed beneath the ills upon him piled.
                                    Byron.

CITRON....*Estrangement.*

Ev'n as one heat another heat expels,
Or as one nail by strength drives out another;
So the remembrance of my former love
Is by a newer object quite forgotten.
      Shakspeare.

Few years have passed since thou and I
 Were firmest friends, at least in name,
And childhood's gay sincerity
 Preserved our feelings long the same.
But now, like me, too well thou know'st
 What trifles oft the heart recall;
And those who once have loved the most
 Too soon forget they loved at all.
And such the change the heart displays,
 So frail is early friendship's reign,
A month's brief lapse, perhaps a day's,
 Will view thy mind estranged again.
If so, it never shall be mine
 To mourn the loss of such a heart;
The fault was Nature's fault, not thine,
 Which made thee fickle as thou art.
As rolls the ocean's changing tide,
 So human feelings ebb and flow;
And who would in a breast confide
 Where stormy passions ever glow?
      Byron.

Tis otherwise decreed, and I submit!
  Alone I guide my bark adown the stream;
Dark is the voyage, around the night-birds flit,
  The waves are tinged by no sweet-smiling beam.
And now I breathe the parting word—Farewell!
  And now, the cords which fondly bind, I sever!
Break from the scenes I once had loved so well,—
  And tear thine image from my heart for ever!
                    J. W. Hanson.

Farewell, Theresa! that cloud which over
  Yon moon this moment gathering we see,
Shall scarce from her pure path have passed, ere thy
    lover
  Swift o'er the wide wave shall wander from thee.
Long, like that dim cloud, I've hung around thee,
  Darkening thy prospects, saddening thy brow;
With gay heart, Theresa, and bright cheek I found
    thee;
  Oh! think how changed, love, how changed art thou
    now!
But here I free thee: like one awaking
  From fearful slumber, this dream thou'lt tell;
The bright moon her spell too is breaking,
  Past are the dark clouds; Theresa, farewell!
                      Moore.

DRAGON PLANT....*You are near a snare.*

He secretly
Puts pirate's colours out at both our sterns,
That we might fight each other in mistake,
That he should share the ruin of us both !
Crown.

His tongue was soft as velvet leaf,
  His poison-fangs concealing ;
But where he stung, the festering wound
  Was past the art of healing.
"Beware of him whose speech is smooth,"
  The mother spake her daughter ;
"The deepest depths are ever found
  Where flows the smoothest water."
"His heart is like an angel's heart,"
  The daughter spake her mother ;
"He seeks to be to thee and me
  A loving son and brother."
She listened to his guileful tale,
  Nor heeded words of warning ;
Ah ! bitterly did future pain
  Repay her present scorning.
For Robin laid his cunning game
  With art so deep and skilful,
That gentle Ellen's mind was turned
  To disobedience wilful.
MacKellar.

Is there no way to save thee? minutes fly,
And thou art lost! *thou!* my sole benefactor,
The only being who was constant to me
Through every change.   Yet, make me not a traitor!
Let me save thee—but spare my honour!

Byron.

Ah, heedless girl! why thus disclose
    What ne'er was meant for other ears?
Why thus destroy thine own repose,
    And dig the source of future tears?
Oh! thou wilt weep, imprudent maid,
    While lurking, envious foes will smile,
For all the follies thou hast said,
    Of those who spoke but to beguile.

Byron.

Again, I tell thee, ask not; but by all
Thou holdest dear on earth or heaven—by all
The souls of thy great fathers, and thy hope
To emulate them, and to leave behind
Descendants worthy both of them and thee—
By all thou hast of blest in hope or memory—
By all thou hast to fear here or hereafter—
By all the good deeds thou hast done to me,
Good I would now repay with greater good,
Remain within—trust to thy household gods
And to my word for safety, if thou dost
As I now counsel—but if not, thou art lost!

Byron.

REED....*Single Blessedness.*

But earlier is the rose distilled,
Than that which withering on the virgin thorn
Grows, lives, and dies in single blessedness.
Shakspeare.

Love not, love not; the thing you love may change;
  The rosy lip may cease to smile on you,
The kindly beaming eye grow cold and strange,
  The heart still warmly beat, and not for you.
Mrs. Norton.

Alone! alone! how drear it is always to be alone!
In such a depth of wilderness, the only thinking one!
The waters in their path rejoice, the trees together
    sleep—
But I have not one silver voice upon my ear to creep!
Willis.

Do any thing but love; or, if thou lovest,
And art a woman, hide thy love from him
Whom thou dost worship. Never let him know
How dear he is; flit like a bird before him;
Lead him from tree to tree, from flower to flower;
But be not won; or thou wilt, like that bird,
When caught and caged, be left to pine neglected,
And perish in forgetfulness.
Miss Landon.

O many a summer's morning glow
   Has lent the rose its ray,
And many a winter's drifting snow
   Has swept its bloom away;
But she has kept the faithless pledge
   To this, her winter hour,
And keeps it still, herself alone,
   And wasted like the flower.
                   O. W. Holmes.

My heart is with its early dream;
   It cannot turn away
To seek again the joys of earth,
   And mingle with the gay.
The dew-nursed flower that lifts its brow
   Beneath the shades of night,
Must wither when the sunbeam sheds
   Its too resplendent light.
My heart is with its early dream,
   And vainly love's soft power
Would seek to charm that heart anew,
   In some unguarded hour.
I would not that some gentle one
   Should hear my frequent sigh;
The deer that bears its death-wound, turns
   In loneliness to die.
                   Mrs. Embury.

Fennel.....*Strength.*

Oh, fear not in a world like this,
  And thou shalt know ere long,
Know how sublime a thing it is,
  To suffer and grow strong.

Longfellow.

As the slow beast with heavy strength indued
In some wide field by troops of boys pursued,
Though round his sides a wooden tempest rain,
Crops the tall harvest, and lays waste the plain;
Thick on his hide the hollow blows resound,
The patient animal maintains his ground,
Scarce from the field with all their efforts chased,
And stirs but slowly when he stirs at last.
On Ajax thus a weight of Trojans hung,
The strokes redoubled on his buckler rung;
Confiding now in bulky strength he stands,
Now turns, and backward bears the yielding bands:
Now stiff recedes, yet hardly seems to fly,
And threats his followers with retorted eye.
Fixed as the bar between two warring powers,
While hissing darts descend in iron showers:
In his broad buckler many a weapon stood,
Its surface bristled with a quivering wood;
And many a javelin, guiltless, on the plain
Marks the dry dust, and thirsts for blood in vain.

Pope.

Thrice sounds the clarion ; lo ! the signal falls,
  The den expands, and expectation mute
Gapes round the silent circle's peopled walls.
  Bounds with one lashing spring the mighty brute,
And, wildly staring, spurns, with sounding foot,
  The sand, nor blindly rushes on his foe :
Here, there, he points his threatening front, to suit
  His first attack, wide waving to and fro
His angry tail ; red rolls his eye's dilated glow.
Byron.

The lusty strength of youth
Is better far than proud decrepitude.
With mind and might and fortitude endued,
  We stand erect and fight for present truth.
We're in the young delight of new existence ;
  The ardent blood leaps lively in our veins ;
The dim traditions glimmering in the distance
  We scorn, for objects worthier manly pains.
MacKellar.

He that of such a height hath built his mind,
And reared the dwelling of his thoughts so strong,
As neither fear nor hope can shake the frame
Of his resolved powers ; nor do all the wind
Of vanity or malice pierce to wrong
His settled peace, or to disturb the same :
What a fair seat hath he, from whence he may
The boundless wastes and weilds of man survey !
Daniel.

Coxcomb....*Singularity.*

Go then, and if you can, admire the state
Of beaming diamonds, and reflected plate;
Procure a taste to double the surprise,
And gaze on Parian charms with learned eyes:
Be struck with bright brocade, or Tyrian dye,
Or birth-day nobles' splendid livery.

Pope.

He also had a quality uncommon
  To early risers after a long chase,
Who wake in winter ere the cock can summon
  December's drowsy day to his dull race,—
A quality agreeable to woman,
  When her soft liquid words run on apace,
Who likes a listener, whether saint or sinner,—
He did not fall asleep just after dinner;
But, light and airy, stood on the alert,
  And shone in the best part of dialogue,
By humouring always what they might assert,
  And listening to the topics most in vogue;
Now grave, now gay, but never dull or pert;
  And smiling but in secret—cunning rogue!
He ne'er presumed to make an error clearer;
In short, there never was a better hearer.

Byron.

GRASS....*Submission.*

ACCORDING to the Greek historians, Grass was made
the symbol of submission, because the ancient nations
of the West gathered Grass and presented it to the conqueror, to show that they confessed themselves overcome.   The grass is trodden under foot by imperial
man; and, instead of returning to its former vigour
with elastic spring, or punishing its violator like the
nettle, yields to its fate—spiritless submission.

It grieves me to the soul
To see how man submits to man's control;
How overpowered and shackled minds are led
In vulgar tracks, and to submission bred.

                                        Crabbe.

You shall be as a father to my youth,
My voice shall sound as you do prompt mine ear;
And I will stoop and humble my intents
To your well practised, wise directions.

                                        Shakspeare.

Romans now
Have thews and limbs like to their ancestors;
But, wo the while! our fathers' minds are dead,
And we are governed with our mother's spirits;
Our yoke and sufferance show us womanish.

                                        Shakspeare.

E'en liberty itself is bartered here.
At gold's superior charms all freedom flies,
The needy sell it, and the rich man buys;
A land of tyrants, and a den of slaves,
Here wretches seek dishonourable graves,
And, calmly bent, to servitude conform,
Dull as their lakes that slumber in the storm.

Goldsmith.

Yet, still the loss of wealth is here supplied
By arts, the splendid wrecks of former pride;
From these the feeble heart and long-fallen mind
An easy compensation seem to find.
Here may be seen, in bloodless pomp arrayed,
The pasteboard triumph and the cavalcade;
Processions formed for piety and love,
A mistress or a saint in every grove.
By sports like these are all their cares beguiled,
The sports of children satisfy the child;
Each nobler aim, repressed by long control,
Now sinks at last, or feebly mans the soul;
While low delights, succeeding fast behind,
In happier meanness occupy the mind:
As in those domes, where Cæsars once bore sway,
Defaced by time and tottering in decay,
There in the ruin, heedless of the dead,
The shelter-seeking peasant builds his shed;
And, wondering man could want the larger pile,
Exults, and owns his cottage with a smile.

Goldsmith

Fir.... *Time.*

What does not fade? the tower, that long had stood
The crush of thunder and the warring winds,
Shook by the slow, but sure destroyer, Time,
Now hangs in doubtful ruins o'er its base,
And flinty pyramids and walls of brass
Descend; the Babylonian spires are sunk;
Achaia, Rome, and Egypt moulder down.
Time shakes the stable tyranny of thrones,
And tottering empires crush by their own weight.

Armstrong.

The clock upon the mantel-piece is ticking;
   Thus hour by hour it tolls a funeral chime:
By day and night its calm and constant clicking
   Denotes the speed of the old traveller Time.
It is a solemn voice.   Who hath an ear
To hear its warning accents, let him hear,
   And preparation make to meet the day
When he, alone, shall lie upon the brink
Of human life, and death shall bid him drink
   The hemlock cup that none can put away.
What though man turn from the unwelcome theme,
   Will Time sit still for man's forgetfulness?—
To watch and wake were wiser than to dream
   And wake at last to wo remediless.

MacKellar.

The world's great age begins anew,
   The golden years return,
The earth doth like a snake renew
   Her winter weeds outworn:
Heaven smiles, and faiths and empires gleam
Like wrecks of a dissolving dream.
  A brighter Hellas rears its mountains
   From waves serener far;
  A new Peneus rolls its fountains
   Against the morning-star.
Where fairer Tempes bloom, there sleep
Young Cyclads, on a sunnier deep;
A loftier Argos cleaves the main,
   Fraught with a later prize;
Another Orpheus sings again,
   And loves, and weeps, and dies.
A new Ulysses leaves once more
Calypso for his native shore.
Oh, write no more the tale of Troy,
   If earth Death's scroll must be!
Nor mix with Laian rage the joy
   Which dawns upon the free:
Although a subtile sphinx renew
Riddles of death Thebes never knew,
Another Athens shall arise,
   And to remoter time
Bequeath, like sunset to the skies,
   The splendour of its prime;
And leave, if naught so bright may live,
All earth can take or heaven can give.
Saturn and Love their long repose
   Shall burst, more wise and good

Than all who fell, than one who rose,
    Than many unwithstood—
Not gold, nor blood, their altar dowers,
But native tears and symbol flowers.
Oh cease! must hate and death return?
    Cease! must men kill and die?
Cease! drain not to its dregs the urn
    Of bitter prophecy.
The world is weary of the past—
Oh, might it die or rest at last!

                                       Shelley.

Time past and time to come are not—
Time present is our only lot;
O God, henceforth our hearts incline
To seek no other love than thine!

                                  Montgomery.

Then haste thee, Time—'tis kindness all
    That speeds thy winged feet so fast;
Thy pleasures stay not till they pall,
    And all thy pains are quickly past.

                                    Bryant.

Time hath, my lord, a wallet at his back,
Wherein he puts alms for oblivion,
A great-sized monster of ingratitudes:
Those scraps are good deeds past: which are de-
    voured
As fast as they are made, forgotten as soon
As done.

                                    Shakspeare.

As through a valley remote I strayed,
Methought, beside a mouldering temple's stone,
The tale of whose dark structure was unknown,
I saw the form of Time: his scythe's huge blade
Lay swathed in the grass, whose gleam was seen
Fearful, as oft the wind, the tussocks green
Moved stirring to and fro: the beam of morn
Cast a dim lustre on his look forlorn;
When touching a responsive instrument,
Stern o'er the chords his furrowed brow he bent:
Meantime a naked boy, with aspect sweet,
Played smiling with the hour-glass at his feet!
Apart from these, and in a verdant glade,
A sleeping infant on the moss was laid,
O'er which a female form her vigils kept,
And watched it, softly-breathing as it slept.
Then I drew nigh, and to my listening ear
Came, stealing soft and slow, this ditty clear:

   "Lullaby, sing lullaby,—
    Sweetest babe, in safety lie;
    I thy mother sit and sing,
    Nor hear of Time the hurrying wing.
    Here, where innocence reposes,
      Fairy sylphs, your sports delay;
    Then the breath of morning roses
      From its bed of bliss convey.
    Lullaby, sing lullaby,—
    Sweetest babe, in safety lie;
    I thy mother sit and sing,
    Nor hear of Time the hurrying wing."

Bowles.

16

Relentless Time! that steals with silent tread,
Shall tear away the trophies of the dead.
Fame, on the pyramid's aspiring top,
With sighs shall her recording trumpet drop;
The feeble characters of Glory's hand
Shall perish, like the tracks upon the sand;
But not with these expire the sacred flame
Of virtue, or the good man's awful name.

Bowles.

O Time! who know'st a lenient hand to lay
   Softest on sorrow's wound, and slowly thence
   (Lulling to sad repose the weary sense)
The faint pang stealest unperceived away;
On thee I rest my only hope at last,
   And think, when thou hast dried the bitter tear
   That flows in vain o'er all my soul held dear,
I may look back on every sorrow past,
And meet life's peaceful evening with a smile—
   As some lone bird, at day's departing hour,
   Sings in the sunbeam, of the transient shower
Forgetful, though its wings are wet the while:—
Yet ah! how much must that poor heart endure,
Which hopes from thee, and thee alone, a cure!

Bowles.

COMMON THISTLE....*Misanthropy.*

Who would seek or prize
    Delights that end in aching?
Who would trust to ties
    That every hour are breaking?
Better far to be
    In utter darkness lying,
Than be blest with light, and see
    That light for ever flying.
All that's bright must fade,—
    The brightest still the fleetest,
All that's sweet was made
    But to be lost when sweetest!

Moore.

I had much rather see
A crested dragon or a basilisk,
Both are less poison to my eyes and nature.

Dryden.

Hate all, curse all: show charity to none;
But let the famished flesh slide from the bone,
Ere thou relieve the beggar: give to dogs
What thou deniest to men; let prisons swallow them,
Debts wither them to nothing: be men like blasted
        woods,
And may diseases lick up their false bloods.

Shakspeare.

I am Misanthropos, and hate mankind:
For thy part, I do wish thou wert a dog,
That I might love thee something.

Shakspeare.

I'll keep my way alone, and burn away—
Evil or good I care not, so I spread
Tremendous desolation on my road:
I'll be remembered as huge meteors are;
From the dismay they scatter.

Proctor.

I see thou art implacable, more deaf
To prayers than winds and seas; yet winds and seas
Are reconciled at length, and sea to shore:
Thy anger, unappeasable, still rages
Eternal tempest never to be calm.

Milton.

Warped by the world in disappointment's school,
In words too wise, in conduct there a fool;
Too firm to yield, and far too proud to stoop,
Doomed by his very virtues for a dupe,
He cursed those virtues as the cause of ill,
And not the traitors who betrayed him still;
Nor deemed that gifts bestowed on better men,
Had left him joy, and means to give again.
Feared, shunned, belied, ere youth had lost her force,
He hated men too much to feel remorse,
And thought the voice of wrath a sacred call,
To pay the injuries of some on all.

Byron.

He has outsoared the shadow of our night;
Envy and calumny, and hate and pain,
And that unrest which men miscall delight,
Can touch him not and torture not again;
From the contagion of the world's slow stain
He is secure, and now can never mourn
A heart grown cold, a head grown gray in vain;
Nor, when the spirit's self has ceased to burn,
With sparkless ashes load an unlamented urn.

Shelley.

They too, who mid the scornful thoughts that dwell
   In his rich fancy, tinging all its streams,
As if the Star of Bitterness which fell
   On earth of old, and touched them with its beams,
Can track a spirit, which, though driven to hate,
From Nature's hands came kind, affectionate;
And which, even now, struck as it is with blight,
Comes out, at times, in love's own native light—
How gladly all, who've watched these struggling rays
Of a bright, ruined spirit through his lays,
Would here inquire, as from his own frank lips,
   What desolating grief, what wrongs had driven
That noble nature into cold eclipse—
   Like some fair orb, that, once a sun in heaven,
And born, not only to surprise, but cheer
With warmth and lustre all within its sphere,
Is now so quenched, that, of its grandeur, lasts
Naught but the wide cold shadow which it casts!

Moore.

   , Dew Plant....*Serenade.*

Inesilla! I am here:
Thy own cavalier
Is now beneath thy lattice playing:
Why art thou delaying?

He hath ridden many a mile
But to see thy smile:
The young light on the flowers is shining,
Yet he is repining.

What to him is a summer star,
If his love's afar?
What to him the flowers perfuming,
When his heart's consuming?

Sweetest girl! why dost thou hide?
Beauty may abide
Even before the eye of morning,
And want no adorning.

Now, upon their paths of light,
Starry spirits bright
To catch thy brighter glance are staying:
Why art thou delaying?
       Barry Cornwall.

Listen! from the forest boughs
  The voice-like angel of the spring
Utters his soft vows
  To the proud rose blossoming.

And now beneath thy lattice dear!
  I am like the bird complaining:
Thou above (I fear)
  Like the rose disdaining.

From her chamber in the skies
  Shouts the lark at break of morning,
And when day-light flies
  Comes the raven's warning.

This of gloom and that of mirth
  In their mystic numbers tell;
But thoughts of sweeter birth
  Teacheth the nightingale.

                              Barry Cornwall.

PINE.....*Pity.*

NAUGHT is there under Heaven's wide hollowness
  That moves more dear compassion of the mind
Than beauty brought to unworthy wretchedness
  Through envy's snares, or fortune's freaks unkind:
  I, whether lately through her brightness blind,
Or through allegiance and vast fealty,
  Which I do owe unto all womankind,
Feel my heart pierced with so great agony,
When such I see, that all for pity I could die.

Spenser.

Like Ariadne, when in pale despair
  The Athenian left her,—so sad Eva pined,
And so she went complaining to the air,
  And gave her tresses to the careless wind:—
  The colour of her fate was on her mind,
Dark, death-like, and despairing;—and her eye
Shone lustrous, like the light of prophecy.

Over the grassy meads,—beside lone streams,
  To perilous heights which no weak step could reach,
She wandered, feeding her unearthly dreams
  With musing, and would move the tremulous beech
  And shuddering aspen with imploring speech;
For nothing that did live, save they (who sighed)
Pitied the downfall of her amorous pride.

Barry Cornwall.

NARCISSUS SCARLET, GERANIUM MARIGOLD

Your self love and stupidity ascite us pity

Has Hope, like the bird in the story,
   That flitted from tree to tree
With the talisman's glittering glory—
   Has Hope been that bird to thee?
On branch after branch alighting,
   The gem did she still display,
And, when nearest and most inviting,
   Then waft the fair gem away!
If thus the sweet hours have fleeted,
   When Sorrow herself looked bright;
If thus the fond hope has cheated,
   That led thee along so light;
If thus, too, the cold world wither
   Each feeling that once was dear ;—
Come, child of misfortune! come hither,
   I'll weep with thee, tear for tear.

                         Moore.

The blind man groping cautiously his way
   Along the crowded pavement of a city,
   Has natural claims upon our tender pity.
Whether 'twere night, or whether it were day,
   Would seem to make small difference to him
   Whose days and nights alike are ever dim ;
Yet still the tramp of human feet, and hum
   Of human voices, sweetly fill his ear ;
   The surgings of the tides of life appear
Like the deep sounds that from the ocean come
   At midnight to the listener.   Pity's glance
Upon his form instinctively we throw ;
   And while some sadness clouds our countenance,
To GOD we pray to save us from such wo.

                         MacKellar.

Come, chase that starting tear away,
　Ere mine to meet it springs;
To-night, at least, to-night be gay,
　Whate'er to-morrow brings!
Like sunset gleams, that linger late
　When all is darkening fast,
Are hours like these we snatch from Fate—
　The brightest and the last.

Moore.

'Tis the last rose of summer,
　Left blooming alone;
All her lovely companions
　Are faded and gone;
No flower of her kindred,
　No rose-bud is nigh,
To reflect back her blushes,
　Or give sigh for sigh!

I'll not leave thee, thou lone one,
　To pine on the stem;
Since the lovely are sleeping,
　Go, sleep thou with them.
Thus kindly I scatter
　Thy leaves o'er the bed,
Where thy mates of the garden
　Lie scentless and dead.

Moore.

SAGE....*Domestic Virtues.*

AT length his lonely cot appears in view,
Beneath the shelter of an aged tree;
Th' expectant wee things, todlin stacher through
To meet their dad, wi' flichtering noise and glee;
His wee-bit ingle blinkin bonilie,
His clean hearth-stane, his thrifty wifie's smile,
The lisping infant prattling on his knee,
Does a' his weary kiaugh and care beguile,
And makes him quite forget his labour and his toil.

Burns.

How warmly we are loved, we seldom learn
   Till pain and sorrow take our strength away;
Then hearts too long estranged, to us will turn,
   And be at peace, as in a former day.
Our true and loving wife more loving grows;
   Our little ones in pitying wonder stand
   Beside the bed and clasp our fevered hand;
Their glistening eye the tear of feeling shows;
   And it may be, when evening calls to rest,
They sadly kneel beside their mother's chair,
Their silvery voices blend in simple prayer,
   And for their sire they make a child's request.
The times of anguish vainly are not given.
That lead a family to unity and heaven.

MacKellar.

Poor madam now condemned to hack
The rest of life with anxious Jack,
Perceiving others fairly flown,
Attempted pleasing him alone.
Jack soon was dazzled to behold
Her present face surpass the old:
With modesty her cheeks are dyed,
Humility displaces pride;
For tawdry finery is seen
A person ever neatly clean;
No more presuming on her sway,
She learns good nature every day;
Serenely gay, and strict in duty,
Jack finds his wife a perfect beauty.

Goldsmith.

Yes! let the rich deride, the proud disdain,
These simple blessings of the lowly train,
To me more dear, congenial to my heart,
One native charm, than all the gloss of art:
Spontaneous joys, where nature has its play,
The soul adopts, and owns their first-born sway;
Lightly they frolic o'er the vacant mind,
Unenvied, unmolested, unconfined.
But the long pomp, the midnight masquerade,
With all the freaks of wanton wealth arrayed,
In these, ere triflers half their wish obtain,
The toiling pleasure sickens into pain:
And e'en while fashion's brightest arts decoy,
The heart distrusting asks, if this be joy?

Goldsmith.

The first sure symptoms of a mind in health,
Is rest of heart, and pleasure felt at home.

Young.

Nor need we power or splendour,—
  Wide hall or lordly dome ;
The good, the true, the tender,—
  These form the wealth of home.

Mrs. Hale.

His warm but simple home, where he enjoys
With her who shares his pleasure and his heart,
Sweet converse.

Cowper.

Home is the sphere of harmony and peace,
The spot where angels find a resting-place,
When, bearing blessings, they descend to earth.

Mrs. Hale.

Home is the resort
Of love, of joy, of peace, and plenty, where,
Supporting and supported, polished friends
And dear relations mingle into bliss.

Thomson.

An angel always dwells beneath the roof
Where, in her virtue, a sweet wife fulfils
Her gentle duties ; and unnumbered ills
From that love-guarded precinct keep aloof.

MacKellar.

LICHEN....*Solitude.*

How use doth breed a habit in a man!
The shadowy desert, unfrequented woods,
I better brook than flourishing peopled towns:
There can I sit alone, unseen of any,
And to the nightingale's complaining notes
Tune my distresses, and record my woes.

Shakspeare.

Full many a dreary hour have I past,
My brain bewildered, and my mind o'ercast
With heaviness; in seasons when I've thought
No sphery strains by me could e'er be caught
From the blue dome, though I to dimness gaze
On the far depth where sheeted lightning plays;
Or, on the wavy grass outstretched supinely,
Pry 'mong the stars, to strive to think divinely:
That I should never hear Apollo's song,
Though feathery clouds were floating all along
The purple west, and, two bright streaks between,
The golden lyre itself were dimly seen:
That the still murmur of the honey-bee
Would never teach a rural song to me:
That the bright glance from beauty's eyelids slanting
Would never make a lay of mine enchanting,
Or warm my breast with ardour to unfold
Some tale of love and arms in time of old.

Keats.

No din
Invades the temple of their mind ;—the mirth
    And sighs of men are sounds to them unknown,
    Though well they know the spirit's inward groan ;
And mortal agonies belong to them
    As well as to their fellow men ; for death
    Hath passed on all who draw the vital breath,
And where sin is, there doth the law condemn.
Ah, hapless men! relentless Silence keeps
    Her watchpost at the portals of the ear ;
    No heavenly word or sound approacheth near
And music's melting influence in lasting stillness sleeps.
                                        MacKellar.

There was a poet whose untimely tomb
No human hands with pious reverence reared,
But the charmed eddies of autumnal winds
Built o'er his mouldering bones a pyramid
Of mouldering leaves in the waste wilderness ;
A lovely youth !—no mourning maiden decked
With weeping flowers, or votive cypress wreath,
The lone couch of his everlasting sleep :
Gentle and brave, and generous, no lorn bard
Breathed o'er his dark fate one melodious sigh :
He lived, he died, he sang, in solitude.
Strangers have wept to hear his passionate notes,
And virgins, as unknown he past, have sighed
And wasted for fond love of his wild eyes.
The fire of those soft orbs has ceased to burn,
And Silence, too, enamoured of that voice,
Locks its mute music in her rugged cell.
                                        Shelley.

How blest the Solitary's lot,
Who, all-forgetting, all-forgot,
  Within his humble cell,
The cavern wild with tangling roots,
Sits o'er his newly-gathered fruits,
  Beside his crystal well!
Or, haply, to his evening thought,
  By unfrequented stream,
The ways of men are distant brought,
  A faint collected dream:
    While praising, and raising
      His thoughts to heaven on high,
    As wand'ring, meand'ring,
      He views the solemn sky.
Than I, no lonely hermit placed
Where never human footstep traced,
  Less fit to play the part;
The lucky moment to improve,
And just to stop, and just to move,
  With self-respecting art:
But ah! those pleasures, loves, and joys
  Which I too keenly taste,
The Solitary can despise,
  Can want, and yet be blest!
    He needs not, he heeds not,
      Or human love or hate,
    Whilst I here must cry here,
      At perfidy ingrate!

                                Burns.

DEATH OF THE FLOWERS.

THE melancholy days are come, the saddest of the
    year,
Of wailing winds, and naked woods, and meadows
    brown and sere.
Heaped in the hollow of the grove, the withered leaves
    lie dead;
They rustle to the eddying gust and to the rabbit's
    tread.
The robin and the wren are flown, and from the shrub
    the jay,
And from the wood-top calls the crow, through all the
    gloomy day.
Where are the flowers, the young fair flowers, that
    lately sprang and stood,
In brighter light and softer airs, a beauteous sister-
    hood?
Alas! they all are in their graves; the gentle race of
    flowers
Are lying in their lonely beds, with the fair and good
    of ours.
The rain is falling where they lie: but the cold No-
    vember rain
Calls not, from out the gloomy earth, the lovely ones
    again.
The wind-flower and the violet, they perished long
    ago,
And the wild-rose and the orchis died, amid the sum-
    mer glow;

17

But on the hill the golden-rod, and the aster in the
    wood,
And the yellow sunflower by the brook, in autumn
    beauty stood,
Till fell the frost from the clear cold heaven, as falls
    the plague on men,
And the brightness of their smile was gone, from up-
    land, glade, and glen.
And now, when comes the calm mild day, as still such
    days will come,
To call the squirrel and the bee from out their winter
    home;
When the sound of dropping nuts is heard, though all
    the trees are still,
And twinkle in the smoky light the waters of the rill,
The south wind searches for the flowers whose fra-
    grance late he bore,
And sighs to find them in the wood and by the streams
    no more.
And then I think of one who in her youthful beauty
    died,
The fair meek blossom that grew up and faded by my
    side:
In the cold moist earth we laid her, when the forest
    cast the leaf,
And we wept. that one so lovely should have a life so
    brief:
Yet not unmeet it was that one, like that young friend
    of ours,
So gentle and so beautiful, should perish with the
    flowers.

                                  Bryant.

Dictionary of Flowers,

WITH THEIR EMBLEMATIC SIGNIFICATIONS.

Acacia.........................Friendship.
——— Rose....................Elegance.
Acanthus.......................The Arts.
Achillea millefolia............War.
Adonis, Flos ....Painful Recollections.
Agrimony..............,.........Thankfulness.
Almond-tree....................Indiscretion.
Aloe............................Grief.
Amaranth.......................Immortality.
Amaryllis......................Pride.
Anemone........................Forsaken.
———, Field...............Sickness.
Angelica ....Inspiration.
Angrec.........................Royalty.
Apple blossom.................Preference.
Ash tree.......................Grandeur.
Asphodel ....My Regrets follow you to
               the Grave.
Aster, China...................Variety.
———————..................After-thought

Balm of Gilead..................Cure.
—— Gentle..................Joking.
Balsam ....Impatience.
Barberry.......................Sourness of temper.
Basil ....Hate.
Beech ....Prosperity.
Bilberry........................Treachery.
Bladder-nut ....Frivolous amusement.
Borage..........................Bluntness.
Box tree........................Stoicism.
Bramble.........................Envy.
Broom ....Humility.
————.........................Ardour.
Buck-bean......................Calm repose.
Bugloss.........................Falsehood.
Bulrush.........................Indiscretion.
Burdock.........................Touch me not.
Buttercup......................Ingratitude.

Cactus, Virginia...............Horror.
Canterbury Bell...............Constancy.
Catchfly ....Snare.
Champignon....................Suspicion.
Cherry tree....................Good education.
Chestnut tree.................Do me justice.
Chicory ....Frugality.
Cinquefoil.....................Beloved daughter.
Circæa..........................Spell.
Clematis........................Artifice.
Clot-bur ....Rudeness.
Clove tree.....................Dignity.
Columbine ....Folly.

Convolvulus, Night...........Night.
Coriander.....................Hidden merit.
Corn...........................Riches.
Cornbottle....................Delicacy.
Cornel Cherry tree...........Durability.
Cowslip, American...........You are my divinity.
Cress..........................Resolution.
Crown Imperial..............Power.
Cuscuta.......................Meanness.
Cypress.......................Mourning.

Daffodil.......................Self-love.
Daisy..........................Innocence.
——, Garden........... ......I share your sentiments.
——, Wild.....................I will think of it.
Dandelion......................The rustic oracle.
Day-Lily, Yellow.............Coquetry.
Dittany ....Childbirth.
Dock, Patience ....Patience.
Dodder.........................Meanness.

Ebony tree ....Blackness.
Eglantine ....Poetry.

Fennel.........................Strength.
Fig............................Longevity.
Fir tree.......................Elevation.
Flax...........................I feel your kindness.
Flower-de-Luce................Flame.
Forget-Me-Not.................Forget me not.
Fraxinella.....................Fire.
Fuller's Teasel................Misanthropy.

Geranium, Pencilled leaf...Ingenuity.
————, Rose-scented......Preference.
————, Scarlet............Stupidity.
————, Sorrowful.........Melancholy mind.
————, Wild...............Steadfast piety.
Grass......................Utility.

Hawthorn....................Hope.
Hazel........................Peace, reconciliation.
Heart's-ease ....Think of me.
Heath.......................Solitude.
Heliotrope, Peruvian.........Devoted attachment.
Hellenium ....Tears.
Hepatica ....Confidence.
Holly.......................Foresight.
Hollyhock...................Ambition.
Honeysuckle................Generous and devoted af-
                          fection.
Hop........................Injustice.
Hornbeam...................Ornament.
Horse-chestnut ....Luxury.
Hortensia ....You are cold.
Hyacinth...................Game, play.

Ice-plant ....Your looks freeze me.
Ipomæa.....................I attach myself to you.
Iris.......................Message.
Ivy........................Friendship.

Jasmine ....Amiableness.
————, Carolina...........Separation.
————, Indian ....I attach myself to you.

Jonquil.............................Desire.
Juniper............................Protection.

Larch ....Boldness.
Larkspur..........................Lightness.
Laurel..............................Glory.
Laurustinus ....I die if neglected.
Lavender..........................Mistrust.
Leaves, Dead....................Sadness, melancholy.
Lilac................................First emotions of love.
——, White......................Youth.
Lily.................................Majesty.
Lily of the Valley.............Return of happiness.
Linden tree......................Conjugal love.
Liverwort.........................Confidence.
London Pride...................Frivolity.
Lotus...............................Eloquence.
Lucern ....Life.

Madder............................Calumny.
Maiden Hair.....................Secrecy.
Mallow ....Beneficence.
Manchineel tree...............Falsehood.
Mandrake.........................Rarity.
Maple..............................Reserve.
Marigold..........................Grief.
————, Prophetic..........Prediction.
———— and Cypress.......Despair.
Marvel of Peru.................Timidity.
Meadow Saffron ....My best days are past.
Mezereon..........................Coquetry.
——————.......................Desire to please.

Mignonette ....Your qualities surpass your
                                charms.
Milkwort..........................Hermitage.
Mistletoe.........................I surmount all difficulties.
Moonwort.........................Forgetfulness.
Moss.............................Maternal Love.
Mulberry tree, Black.........I shall not survive you.
——————, White ....Wisdom.
Musk-plant.......................Weakness.
Myrobolan........................Privation.
Myrtle...........................Love.

Narcissus........................Self-love.
Nettle...........................Cruelty.
Nightshade, Bitter-sweet....Truth.
——————, Enchanter's ...Spell.
Nosegay..........................Gallantry.

Oak..............................Hospitality.
Olive............................Peace.
Ophrys, Spider ....Skill.
Orange Flower................Chastity.
—————— tree...................Generosity.
Orchis, Bee.....................Error.

Parsley ....Festivity.
Passion Flower................Faith.
Peppermint.....................Warmth of feeling.
Periwinkle......................Tender recollections.
Pine-apple ....You are perfect.
Pink.............................Pure love.
——, Yellow..................Disdain.

Plane tree........................Genius.
Plum tree........................Keep your promises.
————, Wild...............Independence.
Poplar, Black.................Courage.
————, White ....Time.
Poppy............................Consolation.
————............................Sleep.
————, White ....My bane, my antidote.
Potato ....Beneficence.
Primrose ....Childhood.
————, large-flowered Even-
  ing...............................Inconstancy.
Privet.............................Prohibition.

Quince............................Temptation.

Ranunculus ....You are radiant with
                                            charms.
Reeds.............................Music.
Rose...............................Love.
————, Hundred-leaved ....Grace.
————, Monthly.................Beauty ever new.
————, Musk.....................Capricious beauty.
————, Single ....Simplicity.
————, White....................Silence.
————, Withered.................Fleeting beauty.
————, Yellow ....Infidelity.
Rosebud..........................A young girl.
————, White ....A heart unacquainted with
                                            love.
Rosemary ....Your presence revives me.
Rue, Wild.......................Morals.

Rush ....Docility.

Saffron ....Beware of excess.
Sage................................Esteem.
Sainfoil, Shaking ....Agitation.
St. John's Wort...............Superstition.
Sardonia ....Irony.
Sensitive Plant.................Chastity.
Snapdragon......................Presumption.
Snowdrop ....Hope.
Sorrel, Wood....................Joy.
Speedwell ....Fidelity.
Spindle-tree......................Your charms are engraven
                          on my heart.
Star of Bethlehem ....Purity.
Stock..............................Lasting beauty.
——, Ten Week...............Promptness.
Stonecrop ....Tranquillity.
Straw, Broken ....Rupture of a contract.
——, Whole....................Union.
Strawberry ....Perfection.
Sunflower ....False riches.
Sweet Sultan...................Happiness.
Sweet William.................Finesse.
Sycamore.........................Curiosity.
Syringa............................Fraternal.

Tansey, Wild...................I declare war against you.
Tendrils of climbing plants.Ties.
Thistle............................Surliness.
Thorn-apple ....Deceitful charms.
Thrift.............................Sympathy.

Thyme..............................Activity.
Tremella Nostoc...............Resistance.
Truffle.............................Surprise.
Tuberose ....Dangerous pleasures.
Tulip................................Declaration of love.
Tussilage, Sweet-scented....Justice shall be done to you.

Valerian...........................An accommodating disposi-
                                tion.
————, Greek...............Rupture.
Venus's Looking-glass.......Flattery.
Veronica..........................Fidelity.
Vervain...........................Enchantment.
Vine................................Intoxication.
Violet.............................Modesty.
———, White ....Innocence, candour.

Wallflower.......................Fidelity in misfortune.
Walnut.............................Stratagem.
Whortleberry..................Treachery.
Willow, Weeping ....Mourning.
Wormwood.....................Absence.

Yew................................Sorrow.

The Calendar of Flowers.

THE Roman Catholic monks, or the observers of the
Roman Catholic ritual, have compiled a Catalogue of
Flowers for every day in the year, and dedicated each
flower to a particular saint, on account of its blooming
about the time of that saint's festival. These appro-
priations form a complete Calendar of the Flowers.

The figures attached express the year in which the
saint died.

JANUARY.

1. Laurustinus, *Vibernum tinus.* St. Faine, or Fan-
chea, an Irish saint of the sixth century.
2. Groundsel, *Senecio vulgaris.* St. Macarius of
Alexandria, 394.
3. Iris, Persian, *Iris Persica.* St. Genevieve, patroness of Paris, 422.
4. Hazel, *Corylus avellana.* St. Titus, disciple of St.
Paul.

5. Hellebore, *Helleborus fœtidus.* St. Simeon Stylites of Rome.
6. Moss, screw, *Tortula rigida.* St. Nilammon.
7. Laurel, Portugal, *Prunus Lusitanica.* St. Kentigerna.
8. Tremella, yellow, *Tremella deliquescens.* St. Gudula, patroness of Brussels.
9. Laurel, common, *Prunus lauro-cerasus,* or common small-fruited cherry. St. Marciana of Rome.
10. Gorse, or Furze, *Ulex Europœus.* St. William of Bourges, 1207.
11. Moss, early, *Bryum hornum.* Swan-neck thread-moss. St. Theodosius.
12. Moss, hygrometric, *Funaria hygrometrica.* St. Arcadius.
13. Yew tree, common, *Taxus bacata.* St. Veronica, a nun of Milan, 1497.
14. Strawberry, barren, *Fragaria sterilis.* St. Hilary, 368.
15. Ivy, *Hedera helix.* St. Paul, the first hermit.
16. Nettle, common red Dead, *Lamium purpureum.* St. Marcellus, Pope.
17. Anemone, garden, *Anemone hortensis.* St. Anthony, patriarch of monks, 251.
18. Moss, four-toothed, *Bryum pellucidum.* St. Prisca, a Roman martyr.
19. Nettle, white Dead, *Lamium album.* St. Martha, a Roman martyr, 270.
20. Nettle, woolly Dead, *Lamium Gargaricum.* St. Fabian, Pope.
21. Hellebore, black, *Helleborus niger.* St. Agnes, a special patroness of purity: beheaded at the age of thirteen, 304.

22. Grass, early whitlow, *Draba verna.* St. Vincent, a Spanish martyr.
23. Peziza, *Peziza acetobolum.* St. Raymond of Penna-fort, 1275.
24. Moss, stalkless, *Phascum muticum.* St. Timothy, disciple of St. Paul, 250.
25. Hellebore, winter, *Helleborus hyemalis.* The Con-version of St. Paul.
26. Butter-bur, white, *Tussilago alba,* or Colt's-foot. St. Polycarp.
27. Moss, earth, *Phascum cuspidatum.* St. Chrysostom.
28. Daisy, double, *Bellis perennis plenus.* St. Margaret of Hungary, 1271.
29. Fern, flowering, *Osmunda regalis.* St. Francis of Sales, 1622.
30. Spleen-wort, *Asplenium trichomanes.* St. Martin.
31. Hart's Tongue, or Spleen-wort, *Asplenium scolopen-drium.* St. Marcella, 410.

FEBRUARY.

1. Moss, lesser water, *Fontinalis minor.* St. Ignatius; and Bay-tree, *Laurus nobilis.* St. Bridget, pa-troness of Ireland.
2. Snow-drop, *Galanthus nivalis.* Purification of the Virgin Mary.
3. Moss, great water, *Fontinalis anti-pyretica,* St. Blase of Armenia, 316.
4. Moss, common hair, or Goldilocks, *Polytrichum commune.* St. Jane, or Queen Joan, 1505.
   Bay, Indian, *Laurus indica.* St. Margaret of England.

5. Primrose, common, *Primula vulgaris.* St. Agatha, a Sicilian martyr.
   Primrose, red, *Primula acaulis.* St. Adelaide, 1015.
6. Hyacinth, blue, *Hyacinthus orientalis.* St. Dorothy, 308.
7. Cyclamen, round-leafed, *Cyclamen coum.* St. Romuald, 1027.
8. Moss, narrow-leafed spring, *Mnium androgynum.* St. John of Matha, 1213.
9. Narcissus, Roman, *Narcissus Romanus.* St. Apollonia, 249.
10. Mezereon, *Daphne mezereon.* St. Scholastica, 543.
    Moss, silky fork, *Mnium heteromallum.* St. Coteris, fourth century.
11. Primrose, red, *Primula verna rubra.* St. Theodora, empress, 367.
12. Anemone, noble Liverwort, *Anemone hepatica.* St. Eulalia of Barcelona.
13. Polyanthos, *Plimula Polyanthus.* St. Catherine de Ricci, 1589.
14. Crocus, yellow, *Crocus mœsiacus,* or *Crocus aureus.* St. Valentine, the lover's saint. He was a priest at Rome, and married there about the year 270.
15. Crocus, cloth of gold, *Crocus sulphureus.* St. Sigifred, bishop of Sweden, 1002.
16. Primrose, lilac, *Primula acaulis plena.* St. Juliana.
17. Crocus, Scotch, *Crocus susianus.* St. Flavian, archbishop of Constantinople, 449.
18. Speedwell, wall, *Veronica vernus arvensis.* St. Simeon, bishop of Jerusalem, 116.
19. Speedwell, field, *Veronica agrestis.* St. Barbatus, patron of Benevento, bishop, 682.

20. Cynoglossum omphalodes, or *C. lusitanicum.* St. Milfred, abbess of Munster.

21. Crocus, white, *Crocus albus.* St. Servianus, bishop, 452.

22. Margaret, herb, *Bellis perennis.* St. Margaret of Cortona, 1297.

23. Apricot tree, *Prunus armeniaca.* St. Milburge of England.

24. Fern, great, *Osmunda regalis.* St. Ethelbert, King of Kent.

25. Peach blossom, *Amygdalus persica.* St. Walburg, abbess of Swabia, Germany.

26. Periwinkle, lesser, *Vinca minor.* St. Victor, seventh century.

27. Lungwort, *Pulmonaria officinalis.* St. Leander, bishop, 596.

28. Crocus, purple, *Crocus vernus.* St. Proterius, patriarch of Alexandria, 557.

MARCH.

1. Leek, common, *Allium porrum.* St. David of Wales, archbishop, 544.

2. Chickweed, dwarf mouse-ear, *Cerastium pumilum.* St. Chad, or Ceada, martyr, under the Lombards, in the sixth century.

3. Marigold, golden fig, *Mesembryanthemum, aureum.* St. Cunegunda, empress, 1040.

4. Chickweed, common, *Alsine media.* St. Casimir, prince of Poland, 1458.

5. Hellebore, green, *Helleborus viridis.* St. Adrian, 309.

6. Lily, Lent, *Pseudo narcissus multiplex.* St. Colette, bishop.

7. Daffodil, early, *Narcissus simplex.* St. Perpetua, martyred under the emperor Severus, 203.

8. Rose, ever-blowing, *Rosa semperflorens.* St. Rosa, of Viterbo, 1261.
Jonquil, great, *Narcissus lætus.* St. Felix, 646.

9. Daffodil, hoop-petticoat, *Narcissus bulbocodium.* St. Catherine of Bologna, 1463.

10. Chickweed, upright, *Veronica triphyllos.* St. Droctavæus, abbot, 580.

11. Heath, Cornish, *Erica vagans.* St. Eulogius of Cordova, 851.

12. Ixia, or crocus-leafed Mistletoe, *Ixia bulbocodium,* or *Viscum albus bulbus.* St. Gregory the Great, prætor of Rome, 574.

13. Heart's Ease, *Viola tricolor.* St. Euphrasia, 410.

14. Bindweed, mountain, *Soldanella alpina.* St. Maud, or Matilda, queen, 968.

15. Colt's-foot, common, *Tussilago farfara.* St. Zachary, pope, 752.

16. Daffodil, nodding, *Narcissus nutans.* St. Julian of Cilicia.

17. Violet, sweet, *Viola odorata.* St. Gertrude, abbess, 626.
Shamrock, White Trefoil, *Trifolium repens.* St. Patrick, apostle of Ireland.

18. Leopard's bane, great, *Doronicum pardalianches.* St. Cyril, archbishop of Jerusalem.

19. Star of Bethlehem, yellow, *Ornithogalum luteum.* St. Joseph, spouse of the Virgin Mary.

20. Violet, dog's, *Viola canina.* St. Wolfram, archbishop of Sens, 720.

18

21. Fumitory, bulbous, *Fumaria bulbosa.* St. Bennet, or Benedict, founder of the Order of Benedict, of Rome, 543.
22. Ficaria verna. St. Catherine of Sweden, abbess, 1381.
23. Daffodil, peerless, *Narcissus incomparabilis.* St. Alphonsus Turibius, archbishop of Lima, 1606.
24. Saxifrage, golden, *Chrysosplenium oppositifolium.* St. Irenæus, bishop of Sirmium, 304.
25. Marigold, *Calendula officinalis.* Annunciation of the Virgin Mary.
26. Henbane, nightshade-leafed, *Hyosciamus scopalia.* St. Braulio, bishop of Saragossa, 646.
27. Jonquil, sweet, *Narcissus odorus.* St. John of Egypt, hermit, 394.
28. Leopard's bane, *Doronicum plantagineum.* St. Priscus, 260.
29. Ox-lip, or great Cowslip, *Primula elatior.* St. Eustatius, abbot, 625.

     Fumitory, *Fumaria officinalis.* St. Jonas, 327.
30. Water-cress, *Cardamine hirsuta.* St. John of Climacus.

     Daffodil, lesser, *Narcissus minor.* St. Zosimus, bishop of Syracuse, 660.
31. Benjamin tree, *Laurus benzoin.* St. Benjamin, deacon, martyr, 424.

APRIL.

1. Mercury, French annual, *Mercurialis annua.* St. Hugh, bishop, 1132.
2. Violet, white, *Viola alba.* St. Francis of Paula, a native of Calabria.

3. Alkanet, evergreen, *Anchusa sempervirens.* St. Agape, 304.

4. Crown Imperial, red, *Fritillaria imperialis.* St. Isidore, bishop of Seville, 636.

5. Crown Imperial, yellow, *Fritillaria imperialis lutea.* Vincent Ferrer, 1419.

6. Hyacinth, starch, *Hyacinthus racemosus.* St. Sixtus I., pope.

7. Anemone, wood, *Anemona nemorosa.* St. Aphraates, fourth century.

8. Ground-ivy, *Glechoma hederacea.* St. Dionysius, bishop of Corinth.

9. Polyanthos, red, *Primula.* St. Mary of Egypt, 421.

10. Violet, pale, *Viola tambrigens.* St. Mechtildes, abbess, fourteenth century.

11. Dandelion, *Leontodon taraxacum.* St. Leo the Great, pope, 461.

12. Saxifrage, great thick-leafed, *Saxifraga crassifolia.* St. Zeno, bishop, 380.

13. Narcissus, green, *Narcissus viridiflorus.* St. Hermenegild, martyr, 586.

14. Borage, common, *Borago officinalis.* St. Lidwina, 1184.

15. Stitchwort, greater, *Stellaria holostea.* St. Peter Gonzales, 1246.

16. Tulip, yellow, *Tulipa sylvestris.* St. Joachim of Sienna, 1305.

17. Arum, Friar's cowl, broad-leafed, *Arum arisarum.* St. Stephen of Citeaux, abbot, 1134.

18. Narcissus, musk, *Narcissus moschatus.* St. Appollonius, 186.

19. Garlic, *Allium ursinum.* St. Leo IX., pope, 1054.

20. Snowflake, spring, *Leucoium vernum*. St. Agnes of Monte Pulciano, 1317.
21. Narcissus, cypress, *Narcissus orientalis albus*. St. Anselm, archbishop of Canterbury.
22. Crowfoot, wood, or Goldilocks, *Ranunculus auricomus*. St. Rufus of Glendaloch.
23. Harebell, *Hyacinthus non scriptus*. St. George the martyr, patron of England.
24. Black thorn, *Prunus spinosa*. St. Fidelis.
25. Tulip, clarimond, *Tulipa præcox*. St. Mark, the Evangelist.
26. Erysimum, yellow, *Erysimum barbarea*. St. Richarius, abbot, 645.
27. Daffodil, great, *Narcissus major*. St. Anastasius, pope, 401.
28. Arum, spotted, *Arum maculatum*. Sts. Didymus and Theodora, 304.
29. Herb, Robert, *Geranium robertianum*. St. Robert, abbot of Molesme, 1110.
30. Cowslip, *Primula veris*. St. Catherine of Sienna, 1380.

MAY.

1. Tulip, Genser, *Tulipa gesnerina*. St. Philip, supposed to have been the first of Christ's Apostles.
   Bachelor's Button, *Lychnis dioica*. St. James the just and the less, apostle, martyred in the tumult in the Temple.
2. Charlock, *Raphanus raphanistrum*, or *Sinapus arvensis*. St. Athanasius, patriarch of Alexandria, 373.

3. Narcissus, poetic, *Narcissus poeticus.* The discovery of the cross, 326.

4. Stock Gilliflower, *Cheiranthus incanus.* St. Monica, mother of St. Augustine.

5. Apple-tree, *Pyrus malus.* Sts. Angelus and Pius V., pope, 1572.

6. Globe Flower, bright yellow, *Trollius europæus.* St. John Damascene, 780.

7. Globe Flower, Asiatic, bright orange, *Trollius asiaticus.* St. John of Beverly.

8. Lily of the Valley, *Convallaria majalis.* St. Selena.

9. Lily of the Valley, *Convallaria multiflora.* St. Gregory of Nazianzen, 389.

10. Peony, slender-leafed, *Pæonia tenuifolia.* St. Comgal, Irish abbot, 601.

11. Asphodel, Lancashire, *Asphodelus luteus.* St. Mammertus, archbishop of Vienna, 477.

12. Iris, German, *Iris Germanica.* St. Germanus, patriarch of Constantinople, 733.

13. Comfrey, common, *Symphytum officinalis.* St. John the silent, bishop, 558.

14. Peony, common, *Pæonia officinalis,* and Peony, coralline, *P. corollina.* St. Pontius, 258.

15. Poppy, Welsh, *Papaver cambricum.* St. Dympna, seventh century.

16. Star of Bethlehem, great *Ornithogalum umbellatum.* St. John Nepomucene, 1383.

17. Poppy, early red, *Papaver argemone.* St. Paschal, 1592.

18. Mouse-ear, or Hawkweed, *Hieracium pilosella.* St. Eric, King of Sweden, 1151.

19. Monk's hood, *Aconitum napellus.* St. Dunstan, archbishop of Canterbury, 988.

20. Horse Chestnut, *Æschylus hippocastanum.* St.
     Bernardine of Sienna, 1444.
21. Ragged Robin, *Lychnis flos cuculi.* St. Felix of
     Cantalicio, 1587.
22. Star of Bethlehem, yellow, *Tragopogon pratensis.*
     St. Yvo, 1303.
23. Lilac, *Springa vulgaris.* St. Julia, fifth century.
24. Poppy, monkey, *Papaver orientale.* St. Vincent of
     Lerins, 450.
25. Herb, Bennet, common, *Geum urbanum.* St. Ur-
     ban, pope, 223.
26. Rhododendron, purple, *Rhododendron ponticum.*
     St. Augustine, archbishop of Canterbury, 604.
     Azalea, yellow, *Azalea pontica.* St. Philip Neri,
     1595.
27. Buttercup, *Ranunculus acris.* St. John, pope, 526.
     Bachelor's Button, yellow, *Ranunculus acris plenus.*
     St. Bede, 735.
28. Iris, lurid, *Iris lurida.* St. Germain, bishop of
     Paris, 576.
29. Blue-bottle, *Centaurea montana.* St. Cyril, about 275.
30. Spearwort, lesser, *Ranunculus flammula.* St. Fer-
     dinand III., confessor, King of Castile and Leon,
     1252.
31. Lily, Yellow Turk's cap, *Lilium pomponium.* St.
     Petronilla, first century.

JUNE.

1. Rose, yellow, *Rosa lutea.* St. Justin, martyr, 167.
2. Pimpernel, common scarlet, *Anagallis arvensis.*
     St. Erasmus, 303.

3. Rose of Meaux, *Rosa provincialis.* St. Cecilius, 211.

4. Indian Pink, *Dianthus chinensis.* St. Quirinus, bishop, 304.

5. Rose, three-leafed China, *Rosa sinica.* St. Boniface, first missionary from England to Friesland; afterwards archbishop of Mentz, and primate of Germany and Belgium, eighth century.

6. Pink, common, *Dianthus deltoides.* St. Norbert, 1134.

7. Centaury, red, *Chironia centaureum.* St. Paul, bishop of Constantinople, 350.

8. Money-wort, Herb Two-pence, or creeping Loosestrife, *Lysimachia nummularia.* St. Medard, bishop, sixth century.

9. Barberry, *Berberis vulgaris.* St. Columba, 597.

10. Iris, bright yellow, *Iris pseudo-acorus.* St. Margaret, queen of Scotland, 1093.

11. Daisy, midsummer, *Crysanthemum leucanthemum.* St. Barnabas, apostle, first century.

12. Rose, white dog, *Rosa arvensis.* St. John, hermit, 1479.

13. Ranunculus, garden, *Ranunculus asiaticus.* St. Anthony of Padua, 1231.

14. Basil, sweet, *Ocimum basilicum.* St. Basil, archbishop, 379.

15. Sensitive plant, *Mimosa sensitiva.* St. Vitus, martyr, fourth century.

16. Rose, moss, *Rosa muscosa.* St. Julietta, martyr, 304.

17. Monkey-flower, yellow, *Mimulus luteus.* St. Nicandeo, about 303.

18. Poppy, horned, *Chelidonium glaucum.* St. Marina, eighth century.
19. La Julienne de Nuit, *Hesperis tristis.* St. Juliana Falconieri, 1340.
20. Poppy, doubtful, *Papaver dubium.* St. Silverius, pope, 538.
21. Bugloss, Viper's *Echium Vulgare.* St. Aloysius, 1591.
22. Canterbury Bell, *Campanula medium.* St. Paulinus, bishop of Nola, 431.
23. Ladies Slipper, *Cypripedium calceolus.* St. Etheldreda, 679.
24. St. John's Wort, *Hipericum pulchrum.* Nativity of St. John the Baptist.
25. Sweet William, *Dianthus barbatus.* St. William of Monte Virgine, 1142.
26. Sowthistle, Alpine hairy blue, *Sonchus cœruleus.* St. Reingarda, 1135.
27. St. John's Wort, perforated, *Hypericum perforatum.* St. John of Montier, sixth century.
28. Cornflower, blue, *Centaurea cyanus.* St. Irenæus, bishop of Lyons, 202.
29. Rattle, yellow, *Rhinanthus crista-galli.* St. Peter the apostle.
30. Cistus, yellow, *Cistus helianthemum.* St. Paul the apostle.

JULY.

1. Agrimony, *Agrimonia eupatoria.* St. Aaron.
2. Lily white, *Lilium candidum.* Virgin Mary.
3. Mallow, common, *Malva sylvestris.* St. Phocas, a gardener, 303.

4. Day Lily, tawny, *Hemerocallis fulva.* St. Ulric, bishop of Augsburg.

5. Rose, double yellow, *Rosa sulphurea.* St. Edana, of Elphin and Tuam.

6. Hawkweed, *Crepis barbata.* St. Julian, anchorite, fourth century.

7. Nasturtium, *Tropæolum majus.* St. Felix, bishop of Nantes, 584.

8. Primrose, evening, *Œnothera biennis.* St. Elizabeth, queen of Portugal, 1336.

9. Sowthistle, marsh, *Sonchus palustris.* St. Everildis.

10. Snapdragon, speckled, *Antirrhinum triphyllum.* Sts. Rufina and Secunda, 257.

11. Lupine, yellow, *Lupinus flavus.* St. James, bishop of Nisibis, 350.

12. Snapdragon, great, *Antirrhinum purpureum.* St. John Gualbert, abbot, 1073.

13. Lupine, blue, *Lupinus hirsutus.* St. Eugenius, bishop, 505.

14. Lupine, red, *Lupinus perennis.* St. Bonaventure, cardinal bishop, 1274.

15. Marigold, Small Cape, purple and white, *Calendula pluvialis.* St. Swithin, bishop, 862.

16. Convolvulus, *Convolvulus purpureus.* St. Eustathius, patriarch of Antioch, 338.

17. Sweet-pea, *Lathyrus odoratus.* St. Marcellina, 397

18. Marigold, autumn, *Chrysanthemum coronarium.* St. Bruno, bishop, 1125.

19. Hawkweed, golden, *Hieracium auranticum.* St. Vincent de Paule, 1660.

20. Dragon's head, Virginian, *Dracocephalus Virginianum.* St. Margaret of Antioch.

21. Lily, Philadelphian, *Lilium Philadelphicum.* St. Praxedes.
22. Lily, African, *Agapanthus umbellatus.* St. Mary Magdalen.
23. Musk flower, *Scabias atro-purpurea.* St. Apollinaris, bishop of Ravenna.
24. Lupine tree, *Lupinus arboreus.* St. Lupus, bishop, 478.
25. Herb Christopher, white, *Actea spicata.* St. Christopher.
26. Chamomile, or Corn Feverfew, *Matricaria chamomilla.* St. Ann, mother of the Virgin Mary.
27. Loose-strife, *Lythrum salicaria.* St. Pantaleon, 303.
28. Groundsel, mountain, *Senecio montanus.* St. Innocent I., pope, 417.
29. Chironia, red, *Chironia centorium.* St. Martha.
30. Mullein, white, *Verbascum lychnitis.* St. Julietta, 303.
31. Mullein, yellow, *Verbascum virgatum.* St. Ignatius of Loyola, founder of the Jesuits, 1556.

AUGUST.

1. Stramony, or Thorn-apple, *Datura stramonium.* St. Peter ad Vincula.
2. Tiger Lily, *Lilium tigrum.* St. Alfrida, 834.
3. Hollyhock, *Althea rosea.* Discovery of the relics of St. Stephen, 415.
4. Bluebell, *Campanula rotundifolia.* St. Dominic, founder of the Friar Preachers, 1221.
5. Lily, Egyptian water, *Nelumbo nilotica.* St. Mary ad Nives.

6. Meadow Saffron, *Colchicum autumnale.*—Transfiguration of our Lord on Mount Tabor.

7. Amaranth, common, *Amaranthus hypochondriacus.* St. Cajetan, 1547.

8. Love-lies-bleeding, *Amaranthus procumbens.* St. Hormisdas.

9. Ragwort, yellow, *Senecio jacobæa.* St. Romanus.

10. Balsam, *Impatiens balsamea.* St. Lawrence, martyr, 258.

11. China Aster, *Aster Chinensis.* St. Susanna, third century.

12. Sowthistle, great corn, *Sonchus arvensis.* St. Clare, abbess, 1253.

13. Groundsel, marsh, Great Fen Ragwort, or Bird's Tongue, *Senecio paludosus.* St. Radigunda.

14. Zinnia, *Zinnia elegans.* St. Eusebius, third century.

15. Virgin's Bower, white, *Clematis vitalba.* Assumption of the Virgin Mary; or the miraculous ascent of her body into heaven.

16. Lily, belladonna, *Amaryllis belladonna.* St. Hyacinth, 1257.

17. Snapdragon, Toadflax, *Antirrhinum linaria.* St. Manus, 275.

18. Marigold, African, *Tagetes erecta.* St. Helen, empress, 382.

19. Timothy grass, branched Cat's Tail grass, *Phleum panniculatum,* or *Ph. asperum.* St. Timothy, 304.

20. Dandelion, *Leontodon serotinus.* St. Bernard, abbot, 1153.

21. Marigold, French, *Tagetes patula.* St. Jean Francois de Chantal, 1641.

22. Timothy, common Cat's Tail grass, *Phleum pra-*
tense. St. Timothy, 311.
23. Tansy, common, *Tanacetum vulgare.* St. Philip
Beniti, 1285.
24. Sunflower, tall, *Helianthus annuus.* St. Bartholo-
mew, apostle.
25. Sunflower, perennial, *Helianthus multiflorus.* St.
Louis, king of France, 1270.
26. Amaryllis, banded, *Amaryllis rotata.* St. Zephy-
rinus, pope, 219.
27. Hawkweed, hedge, *Hieracium umbellatum.* St.
Cæsarius, archbishop of Arles, 542.
28. Golden rod, *Solidago Virga aurea.* St. Augustine,
bishop, 430.
29. Hollyhock, yellow, *Althea flava.* St. Sabinus, king,
about 697.
30. Lily, Guernsey, *Amaryllis sarniensis.* St. Rose of
Lima, 1617.
31. Pheasant's eye, *Adonis autumnalis.* St. Raymond
Nonnatus, 1240.

SEPTEMBER.

1. Orpine, or Livelong, great, *Sedum telephium.* St.
Giles, patron of beggars and cripples. Born at
Athens; abbot of Nismes, in France, died 750.
2. Golden rod, *Solidago.* St. Margaret, thirteenth
century.
3. Flea-bane, common yellow, *Inula dysenterica.* St.
Simeon Stylites, the younger, 592.
4. Soapwort, pale pink, *Saponaria officinalis.* St.
Rosalia, 1160.

5. Mushroom, or champignon, *Agaricus campestris.*
   St. Laurence Justinian, first patriarch of Venice.
   1455.
6. Dandelion, *Leontodon autumnalis.* St. Pambo of
   Nitria, 385.
7. Starwort, golden, *Aster solidaginoides.* St. Cloud,
   560.
8. Starwort, Italian blue, *Aster amellus.* St. Adrian,
   306.
9. Golden rod, Canadian, *Solidago Canadensis.* St.
   Omer, 607.
10. Crocus, autumnal, *Crocus autumnalis.* St. Pulche-
    ria, empress, 453.
11. Meadow Saffron, variegated, *Colchicum variegatum.*
    St. Hyacinthus, 257.
12. Passion-flower, semilunar, *Passiflora peltata.* St.
    Earnswith, abbess, seventh century.
13. Crocus, officinal, *Crocus sativus.* St. Eulogius, pa-
    triarch of Alexandria, 608.
14. Passion-flower, blue, *Passiflora cœrulea.* Exaltation
    of the Holy Cross, 629.
15. Saffron Byzantine, *Colchicum Byzanticum.* St.
    Nicetas, fourth century.
16. Starwort, sea-blue, *Aster tripolium.* St. Editha, 984.
17. Mallow, narrow-leafed, *Malva angustifolia.* St.
    Lambert, bishop, 709.
18. Starwort, pendulous, *Aster pendulus.* St. Thomas,
    archbishop of Valencia, 1555.
19. Scabius, Devil's bit, *Scabiosa succisa.* St. Lucy,
    1090.
20. Meadow Saffron, common, *Colchicum autumnale.*
    St. Eustachius.

21. Passion-flower, fringed-leafed, variegated, *Passiflora ciliata*. St. Matthew, the Evangelist.
22. Boletus, tree, *Boletus arboreus*. St. Maurice, fourth century.
23. Starwort, white bushy, *Aster dumosus*. St. Thecla, first century.
24. Fungus, *Agaricus fimetarius*. St. Gerard, bishop, 1046.
25. Boletus, great, order Fungi, *Boletus bovinus*. St. Ceolfrid, abbot, 716.
26. Golden rod, great, *Solidago gigantea*. St. Justina, 304.
27. Starwort, white small-leafed N. American, *Aster multiflorus*. St. Delphina, 1323.
28. Golden rod, evergreen, *Solidago sempervirens*. St. Eustochium, 419.
29. Michaelmas Daisy, *Aster tradescanti*. St. Michael and all angels.
30. Amaryllis, golden, *Amaryllis aurea*. St. Jerome, · 420.

OCTOBER.

1. Amaryllis, lowly, *Amaryllis humilis*. St. Remigius, bishop of Rheims, 533.
2. Soapwort, *Saponaria officinalis*. Feast of the holy guardian angels.
3. Helenium, downy, *Helenium pubescens*. St. Dionysius, the Areopagite, 51.
4. Southernwood, dwarf, *Artemisa abrotanum*. St. Francis of Assissi, founder of the order of Franciscans, 1226.

5. Chamomile, starlike, a fungus, *Boltonia asteroides.* St. Placidus, 546.

6. Feverfew, creeping rooted, *Pyrethrum serotinum.* St. Bruno, founder of the Carthusian order, 1101.

7. Chrysanthemum, Indian, *Chrysanthemum Indicum.* St. Mark, pope, 336.

8. Maudlin, sweet, *Achillea ageratum.* St. Bridget, 1373.

9. Mushroom, milky, *Agaricus lactifluus acris,* or *A. Listeri.* St. Denys, patron saint of France.

10. Aletris, Cape waved-leafed, *Aletris viridifolia.* St. Francis Borgia, 1572.

11. Holly, common, *Ilex aquifolium.* St. Ethelburga, 664.

12. Fleabane, wavy, *Inula undulata.* St. Wilfred, bishop of York, 709.

13. Helenium, yellow, smooth, *Helenium autumnale.* St. Edward, king and confessor, 1066.

14. Fleabane, Indian, *Inula Indica.* St. Calixtus, pope, 222.

15. Sweet Sultan, purple, *Centaurea moschata.* St. Teresa, 1582.

16. Yarrow, *Achillea millefolium.* St. Gall, abbot, 646.

17. Sunflower, dwarf, *Helianthus indicus.* St. Anstrudis, 688.

18. Mushroom, *Agaricus floccosus.* St. Luke, Evangelist, 63.

19. Tick-seed, perennial, *Coreopsis procera.* St. Frideswith, patroness of Oxford, eighth century.

20. Sweet Sultan, yellow, *Centaurea suaveolens.* St. Artemius, 362.

21. Silphium, hairy-stalked, *Silphium asteriscus*. St. Ursula, fifth century.
22. Silphium, rough three-leafed, *Silphium trifoliatum*. St. Nunilo, 840.
23. Starwort, slender-stalked, *Aster junceus*. St. Theodoret, 362.
24. Starwort, Carolina, *Aster Carolinus flexuosus*. St. Proclus, archbishop of Constantinople, 447.
25. Starwort, fleabane, *Aster Conizoides*. St. Crispin, 287.
   Starwort, meagre, *Aster miser*. St. Crispinian, 287.—These were brothers and martyrs, shoemakers, and patrons of that art.
26. Golden rod, late flowered, *Solidago petiolaris*. St. Evaristus, pope, 112.
27. Starwort, floribund, *Aster floribundus*. St. Frumentius, apostle of Ethiopia, fourth century.
28. Chrysanthemum, late-flowering creeping. *Chrysserotinum*. St. Simon, Apostle, the Zealot.
   Starwort, scattered, *Aster passiflorus*. St. Jude, Apostle.
29. Narcissus, green autumnal, *Narcissus viridiflorus*. St. Narcissus, bishop of Jerusalem, second century.
30. Mushroom, mixed, *Agaricus fimetarius*. St. Marcellus the centurion, 298.
31. Tick-seed, fennel-leaved, *Coreopsis ferulafolia*. St. Quintin, 287.

NOVEMBER.

1. Laurustinus, *Laurustinus sempervirens*. St. Fortunatus.

2. Cherry, winter, *Physalis*. St. Marcian, 387.
3. Primrose, *Primula vulgaris*. St. Flour, 389.
4. Strawberry tree, *Arbutus*. St. Brinstane, bishop of Winchester, 931.
5. Cherry, common winter, *Physalis alkakengi*. St. Bertille, abbess of Chelles, 692.
6. Yew tree, common, *Taxus baccata*. St. Leonard, sixth century.
7. Furcræa, *Furcræa gigantea*. St. Willebord, first bishop of Utrecht, 738.
8. Aletris, Cape, *Veltheimia*. The four crowned Brothers, martyrs, 304.
9. Aletris, glaucous-leafed, *Veltheimia glauca*. St. John Lateran.
10. Fir, Scotch, *Pinus sylvestris*. St. Nympha, fifth century.
11. Pine, Weymouth, *Pinus strobus*. St. Martin, bishop, 397.
12. Aloe, great orange-flowering, *Veltheimia*, or *Aletris uvaria*. St. Nilus, 390.
13. Bay, *Laurus poetica*. St. Homobonus, 1197.
14. Laurel, Portugal, *Cerasus Lusitanica*. St. Lawrence, bishop of Dublin, 1180.
15. Colt's foot, sweet-scented, *Tussilago fragrans*. St. Gertrude, abbess, 1292.
16. Hemp, African bow-string, *Sanseviera Guineensis*. St. Edmund, archbishop of Canterbury,.1242.
17. Stramony, or Thorn-apple tree, *Datura arborea*. St. Gregory, Thaumaturgus, bishop, 270.
18. Passion-flower, notch-leafed, *Passiflora serratifolia*. Dedication of the churches of St. Peter and St. Paul at Rome.

19

19. Passion-flower, apple-fruited, *Passiflora maliformis.*
St. Elizabeth of Hungary, 1231.
20. Stapelia, red, *Stapelia rubra.* St. Edmund, king
and martyr, 870.
21. Sorrel, wood, *Oxalis grandiflora.* Presentation of
the Virgin Mary.
22. Sorrel, wood, tube-flowered, *Oxalis tubiflora.* St.
Cecilia, martyr, and patroness of music, particularly of sacred music; supposed to be the
inventress of the organ, 230.
23. Sorrel, convex, *Oxalis convexula.* St. Clement,
pope, 100.
24. Stapelia, starry, *Stapelia radiata.* St. John of the
Cross, 1591.
25. Butterbur, sweet, *Tussilago fragrans.* St. Catherine, patroness of spinsters, third century.
26. Sorrel, linear, *Oxalis linearis.* St. Conrad, bishop
of Constance, 976.
27. Sorrel, lupine-leafed, *Oxalis lupinifolia.* St. Virgil,
bishop of Salzburg, 784.
28. Stapelia, variegated, *Stapelia variegata.* St. Stephen
the younger, 764.
29. Sphenogyne, *S. piloflora.* St. Saturninus, bishop, 257.
30. Sorrel, three-coloured, *Oxalis tricolor.* St. Sapor,
bishop.

DECEMBER.

1. Stapelia, dark, *S. pulla.* St. Eligius, bishop of
Noyon, 659.
2. Geodorum, lemon, *Geodorum citrinum.* St. Bibiania,
363.

3. Indian tree, *Euphorbia tirucalle*. St. Francis Xavier, 1552.

4. Gooseberry, Barbadoes, *Cactus pereskia*. St. Chrysologus, 450.

5. Hibiscus, long-stalked, *H. pedunculatus*. St. Crispina, 304.

6. Heath, nest-flowered, *Erica nudiflora*. St. Nicholas, archbishop of Myra, 342.

7. Achania, hairy, *Achania pilosa*. St. Ambrose, 397.

8. Arbor Vitæ, American, *Thuga occidentalis*. Blessed Virgin Mary.

9. Spruce, Corsican, *Pinus laricio*. St. Leodocia, 304.

10. Cypress, Portugal, *Cupressus pendula*. St. Eulalia.

11. Pine, Aleppo, *Pinus halapensis*. St. Damascus, pope, 384.

12. Heath, crowded, *Erica abietina*. St. Eadburga, 751.

13. Arbor Vitæ, African, *Thuga cupressoides*. St. Lucy, martyr of Syracuse, 304.

14. Pine, swamp, *Pinus palustris*. St. Spiridion, archbishop, 348.

15. Pine, pitch, *Pinus resinosa*. St. Florence, abbot.

16. Arbor Vitæ, Chinese, *Thuga orientalis*. St. Adelaide, empress, 999.

17. Cedar, white, *Cupressus thyoides*. St. Olympias, 410.

18. Cypress, New-Holland, *Cupressus australis*. St. Winebald, 760.

19. Heath, two-coloured, *Erica bicolor*. St. Samthana, abbess, 738.

20. Stone-pine, *Pinus pinea*. St. Philogonius, bishop of Antioch, 322.

21. Sparrow-wort, *Erica passerina*. St. Thomas, apostle.

22. Heath, pellucid, *Erica pellucida.* St. Cyril, 881.
23. Cedar of Lebanon, *Pinus cedrus.* St. Victoria, 250.
24. Pine, frankincense, *Pinus tœda.* Sts. Thrasilla and Emiliana.
25. Holly, *Ilex aculeata baccifera.* Nativity of our Saviour.
26. Heath, purple, *Erica purpurea.* St. Stephen, first martyr.
27. Heath, flame, *Erica flammea.* St. John, the Evangelist.
28. Heath, bloody-flowered, *Erica cruenta.* The Holy Innocents, who suffered from Herod's cruelty.
29. Heath, *Erica genistopha.* St. Thomas, archbishop of Canterbury, 1170.
30. Ponthieva, glandular, *Ponthieva glandulosa.* St. Anysia, 304.
31. There is no flower appropriated to this day.

The Dial of Flowers.

'TWAS a lovely thought to mark the hours,
  As they floated in light away,
By the opening and the folding flowers
  That laugh to the summer's day.

Thus had each moment its own rich hue,
  And its graceful cup and bell,
In whose coloured vase might sleep the dew,
  Like a pearl in an ocean shell.

To such sweet signs might the time have flowed,
  In a golden current on,
Ere from the garden, man's first abode,
  The glorious guests were gone.

So might the days have been brightly told—
  Those days of song and dreams—
When shepherds gathered their flocks of old
  By the blue Arcadian streams;

———

So, in those isles of delight, that rest
    Far off in a breezeless main,
Which many a bark with a weary guest
    Has sought, but still in vain.

Yet is not life, in its real flight,
    Marked thus—even thus—on earth,
By the closing of one hope's delight,
    And another's gentle birth?

Oh! let us live so that, flower by flower,
    Shutting in turn, may leave
A lingerer still for the sunset hour,
    A charm for the shaded eve!

                              Hemans.

When a plant is approaching its state of perfection, when its organs of nourishment are completely developed, and its vegetation is most luxuriant, then arrives the time of flowering, which has been aptly termed "the joy of plants." The most superficial observer must have noticed how different is the season of flowering of individual plants, and how each month is adorned with its particular flowers. When the intense cold of January confines us to our houses, the Black Hellebore, or Christmas Rose, unfolds its dazzling white blossoms; in February, the innocent Snowdrop presents to us her elegant cup. In the same month the Hazel puts forth its catkins, and not rarely the early-blooming Crowfoot shows the blue tips of its clusters of blossom. March boasts a richer Flora; then the Violet delights us with its fragrance; the Mezereon offers its peach-

coloured flowers, and the Primrose leads on a long
train of the charming children of Spring. These now
continue to advance in increasing numbers, displaying,
especially in May and June, their highest splendour;
till at length the Meadow Saffron takes leave of in-
clement Autumn, and, saturated with rain, the Mosses
acquire fresh vigour, and open to the botanist a new
field for investigation.

Not less different than the period of flowering is the
time of the opening and shutting of flowers. Some
plants habitually open and close their flowers by turns;
others are governed in these respects by the weather;
others again, by the length or shortness of the day:
while some open and shut at certain hours, and thus
furnish materials for composing the Dial of Flowers.

According to the observations of later botanists, the
flowery crown of plants serves, among other things, to
envelop the tender organs of fructification, and to pro-
tect them from the pernicious influence of external
agents. Those organs of fructification are the chief
objects of the maternal care of Nature; while shut up
in the flower-bud, they acquire that strength and perfection of parts which enable them to endure the light
of the sun, and to perform the functions for which they
are designed. It is not till they are capable of fulfilling
these functions that the flower unfolds itself; but it
again closes at such times when external influences
might be injurious to the delicate organs of fructification. Many flowers can bear only the refreshing morning air and the first rays of the sun, but remain shut
all the rest of the day. This may be particularly observed in the different species of Convolvulus, Ipomœa,

and Goat's Beard. We find these, in general, open only till about eleven o'clock. In like manner, the Mallows and the Mesembryanthemums unfold their flowers about noon: and precisely at that time, in serene weather, open the singularly-formed Drosera, and the common Purslain, which shut again in an hour. Others unfold themselves only in the evening, and continue open all night, probably because their delicate organs would be injured by the sun. The Œnotheras, the Gauras, and the different species of the Mirabilis, furnish examples of this kind. Thus, too, the Cactus opuntia opens its magnificent blossoms at night only, and towards morning shuts them up for ever. The flowers of many plants of the nineteenth class are observed to hang their heads during night—the Camellia, for example—by which means the rain, or dew, which might injure the tender organs of fructification, can run off the more easily. In other plants of this class, the flower shuts up against rain, and on the approach of evening, as is the case with the Marigolds.

The periodical change of colour in some flowers is also worthy of remark. Thus, the flowers of the speckled French Honeysuckle (*Hedysarum maculatum*) are purple in the morning and green at noon. The changeable Hibiscus (*Hibiscus mutabilis*) is white in the morning, flesh-coloured at noon, and rose-red in the evening. Thus, too, the great Corn-flag (*Gladiolus grandis*) changes its colour several times in the course of the day.

Neither is the scent of flowers equally strong and agreeable at all hours of the day: many, even of our indigenous flowers, have the strongest scent at night.

The *Ixia cinnamomea* gives out its fragrance in the evening only; the highly-scented Lesser Orpine (*Crassula odoratissima*) only in the night; the *Epidendrum fragrans*, morning and evening; another species of Epidendrum, hung up in a room, without earth or water, yields an agreeable perfume for years. The flowers of the *Hebenstreitia dentata* are scentless in the morning, have a disagreeable smell at noon, and give out in the evening a fragrant odour, not unlike that of the Hyacinth.

These properties of flowers, and the opening and shutting of many at particular times of the day, led to the idea of planting them in such a manner as to indicate the succession of the hours, and to make them supply the place of a watch or clock. Those who are disposed to try the experiment may easily compose such a dial by consulting the following table, comprehending the hours between three in the morning and eight in the evening.

Names of Plants.	Hours of Opening.	Hours of Shutting.
Yellow Goat's Beard (*Tragopogon luteum*)........................	3	
Common Base Hawkweed, (*Crepis tectorum*)	4	
Field Sowthistle, (*Sonchus agrestis*)	5	
Dandelion (*Leontodon Taraxacum*)........................	5	
Alpine Base Hawkweed, (*Crepis alpina*)	5	
Naked-stalked Poppy (*Papaver nudicaule*)........................	5	
Orange Day-lily (*Hemerocallis fulva*)........................	5	
Red Hawkweed (*Hieracium rubrum*)........................	5—6	
Meadow Goatmore (*Hypochæris pratensis*)	6	
Red Base Hawkweed, (*Crepis rubra*)........................	6½	
White Water Lily (*Nymphæa alba*)........................	7	
White Spiderwort (*Anthericum album*)........................	7	
Tongue-leafed Mesembryanthemum (*M. linguiforme*)...........	7—8	
Bearded Mesembryanthemum (*M. barbatum*)	8	
Dandelion (*Leontodon Taraxacum*)	...	8—9
Yellow Goat's Beard (*Tragopogon luteum*)........................	...	9
Field Marigold (*Calendula arvensis*)	9	
Single-flowered Hawkweed (*Hieracium Pilosella*)	9	
Red Pink (*Dianthus prolifer*).....	9	

Names of Plants.	Hours of Opening.	Hours of Shutting.
Red Sandwort (*Arenaria rubra*)	10	
Ice Plant (*Mesembryanthemum crystallinum*).....................	10	
Common Base Hawkweed (*Crepis tectorum*)......................	...	11
Alpine Base Hawkweed, (*Crepis alpina*)	...	11
Field Sowthistle (*Sonchus agrestis*)	...	12
Red Pink (*Dianthus prolifer*)......	...	1
Red Base Hawkweed (*Crepis rubra*)	...	1
Bearded Mesembryanthemum (*M. barbatum*)...................	...	2
Single-flowered Hawkweed (*Hieracium Pilosella*).................	...	2
Red Sandwort (*Arenaria rubra*).........	...	8
Field Marigold (*Calendula arvensis*)...........................	...	8
Tongue-leafed Mesembryanthemum (*M. linguiforme*)	...	8
Red Hawkweed (*Hieracium rubrum*)......................	...	4
Ice Plant (*Mesembryanthemum crystallinum*)......	...	4
White Spiderwort, (*Anthericum album*)	...	4
Meadow Goshmore (*Hypochæris pratensis*)	...	5
White Water Lily (*Nymphœa alba*)........................	...	6
Naked-stalked Poppy, (*Papaver nudicaule*)	...	7
Orange Day-lily, (*Hemerocallis fulva*)...........................	...	8

It is, of course, impossible to ensure the accurate going of such a dial, because the temperature, the dryness, and the dampness of the air, have a considerable influence on the opening and shutting of flowers.

THE END.

Lightning Source UK Ltd.
Milton Keynes UK
UKOW030626021211

183035UK00001B/23/A

9 781103 107216